BLOODY B
HISTO

CHELMSFORD

CW00408941

BLOODY BRITISH HISTORY
HISTORY

CHELMSFORD

ROBERT HALLMANN

The
History
Press

To my familiars, Minna and Theo

The History Press
The Mill, Brimscombe Port
Stroud, Gloucestershire, GL5 2QG
www.thehistorypress.co.uk

British Library Cataloguing in Publication Data.
A catalogue record for this book is available from the British Library.

ISBN 978 0 7524 7115 0

Typesetting and origination by The History Press
Printed in Great Britain

CONTENTS

INTRODUCTION

CHELMSFORD, THE PLACE that died and was reborn. The Romans called it Caesaromagus, 'Caesar's Market', a place of commerce. Or maybe, as some say, the name means Caesar's Field, a site where, in AD 43, Emperor Claudius and his elephant-supported legions tramped and fought their way through. Even if you are the leader of a dominant and dominating empire, the only place to be is Essex.

Claudius' triumphal visit provided roads and influence and secured exports from Albion Insula Britannica on the edge of the Roman world for some 400 years. Britain was Romanised to a large degree, but the Romans left and Caesar's market left with them, or so it seems. We hear little of Chelmsford in the land of the Trinovantes until the Bishop of London got permission by Royal Charter to hold a market in *skelmeresford*. Commerce raised the town again, and then jurisprudence was added …

Maybe it never died. Maybe there always was a trading post by the confluence of the rivers Chelmer and Cann? Maybe the fording place was a site that just naturally attracted itinerant people in its central position among the East Saxons, a place that grew and developed organically out of the very soil of history?

As for crime and punishment, law and religion, Chelmsford, the seat of the Essex Assizes with court and gaol, has seen it all. The good, the bad and the ugly have passed through its streets, its many inns – and sometimes to its gallows, and even to a fiery stake. Every kind of evil or wrongdoing has been discussed in its courts and almost every imaginable punishment has been meted out. Witches were hanged and heretics burnt. The worst and the best of judges have sat in judgment.

On the face of it not much has happened, but scratch the surface and all of humanity and its foibles are here. A bishop started a market. Henry VIII built a palace, which Cromwell later bought for a guinea. Queen Mary I spent much of her youth here. The Black Death visited, as did Richard II, and Elizabeth I. Soldiers behaved badly. Some were accidentally burnt – or maybe not accidentally!

And yet, in a largely agricultural area, Chelmsford attracted some surprising innovators in industry. That meant it also attracted Hitler's bombs …

Chelmsford has seen much history and much human tragedy unfold in its courts. There are so many stories …

Robert Hallmann, 2012

Chelmsford has been awarded City status by Queen Elizabeth II on the occasion of her Diamond Jubliee. Hearty congratulations are in order.

ACKNOWLEDGEMENTS

I OWE A HEARTY 'Thank You' to Karen Bowman for her help and diligent research into some of the hidden notes to Chelmsford's history. Nick Wickenden and Dr Mark Curteis from Chelmsford Museum deserve thanks for their help and support, as does Tom Warmington of New Hall School. I must not forget my daughter Tessa and the many people in libraries and collections who added to the illustrations and information (especially www.witchtrials.co.uk).

10,000 BC

MYSTERIES OF PRE-HISTORY

THE CURSUS AT SPRINGFIELD BARNES

Essex has been a home – of a kind – to humans since the Palaeolithic period. The first signs date back to nearly 500,000 BC. Flint artefacts, tools (and waste flakes from their manufacture) have been found in the rich and fertile river valley hunting grounds.

Major ceremonial monuments were built, sacred gathering places where the hunters and foragers could meet annually. Chelmsford had its importance even then. Aerial photography revealed one of these mysterious earthworks, a linear enclosure about 670m long and 40m wide, right on Chelmsford's doorstep – the 'cursus' close by the Chelmer at Springfield Barnes (now Chelmer Village).

All kinds of theories have been advanced in the past to explain their origins and functions. Today, cursus monuments are understood to be Neolithic and therefore probably the oldest monumental structures of the British Isles, older than Stonehenge and the great pyramids of Egypt. With their sometimes massive scale and permanence within the landscape, such monuments have long been shrouded in mystery. Eighteenth-century archaeologists suggested they might be Roman race tracks, based on their shape and size, so they named them 'cursus' – but the Romans came to Britain nigh on 2,000 years ago, only a lifetime or two after the birth of Christ, and cursuses were built some 3,500 years before that.

Older than the Pyramids. An artist's impression of the cursus at Neolithic Springfield. (© Essex County Council)

What was it that happened in those mysterious structures? What was their function? Digging such monuments with the crude implements available – usually the antlers or shoulder blades of large mammals – would need a planned, organised and concerted effort, possibly over several seasons. Investigations between 1979 and 1985 discovered pottery, urn sherds and flint artefacts ranging from the Middle Neolithic era to the early 2nd millennium, 3,500-2,000 BC, indicating that a great deal of feasting took place here. The urn sherds denote burials nearby, all evidence of a prolonged period of use. Fire was a part of the ceremonies – small pits in the interior contained charcoal and burnt flints.

So what was the function of these monuments? Recent studies suggest they were in fact sites for ceremonial competitions. Finds of arrowheads point to archery and hunting, and the length of the cursus may reflect its use as a proving ground for young men in races and other tests of prowess in combat with spears and arrows.

Where swords were made. Springfield Lyons Late Bronze Age enclosure as it may have looked when bronze was cast here. (© Essex County Council)

SPRINGFIELD LYONS' LATE BRONZE AGE ENCLOSURE

Much nearer in time, about 1000-700 BC, circular causewayed enclosures were being constructed as ancestral gathering places. They were somewhere that the normally dispersed itinerant groups could meet up, make contact, bury the dead, hold feasts, and exchange information on the movement of herds; quite important for hunter-gatherers who followed wild horses, wild cattle, deer and elk on their annual migration routes.

Such enclosures were large circular earthworks, two of which were constructed at Great Baddow and at Springfield Lyons, the latter overlooking the Chelmer valley. This roughly circular site, about 60m in diameter, included a deep ditch and rampart, impressive gate structures and several post-hole structures. The principal entrance directly faced the Neolithic cursus. A roundhouse once stood in its centre.

During excavation, proof of what must be the earliest Chelmsford industry was found – the largest quantity of clay moulds for casting bronze of any Bronze Age site in Britain. These date from around 850 BC, though bronze manufacture began in about 2000 BC. Bronze Age swords were usually around 75cm long, and were designed to be strong but flexible (so that they would bend in battle, rather than break).

Bronze Age peoples tamed and rode horses, and wove cloth to supplement their fur outfits. Fashion was beginning to be invented. Bronze Age women held their hair together with bone pins and wore crescent-shaped necklaces.

The Iron Age was represented at the site by a 'broken' sword, found in a pit in the centre of the circular area, and a more mysterious find further to the west of the pit: a horse's head with bridle. Just the skull, an iron bit and two studs remained ... An Iron Age Godfather, perhaps?

The early Saxon period added a cemetery: corpses were cremated here from AD 425-650, and buried here from AD 450-599 (the first being a pagan tradition and the second a Christian one). The graves contain intricate metal jewellery. A town was then built here in the tenth and eleventh centuries, a small settlement of at least thirteen buildings. The largest feature excavated was a hall, a Saxon longhouse measuring 20m long and 6m wide. Today the site is surrounded by houses and a retail park. Down the road, starting from the Asda car park, lies the Neolithic cursus.

It would have been an impressive sight in its day.

CHELMSFORD'S WOOLLY MAMMOTH

It may be difficult to imagine, but this area was once woolly mammoth country. A lower jawbone of the enormous shaggy creature was found right in the middle of Chelmsford, in a brick pit between New London Road and the railway. It is in Chelmsford Museum now.

Britain would have been a less hospitable place then, in a vast, frozen, northern landscape of Arctic tundra that took in much of the North Sea. In the bitter cold the elephant-related mammoths used to roam in large herds, no doubt for warmth and safety in numbers. Humans arrived in England around 500,000 years ago, when they would have wandered over from the Continent before the Channel flooded and separated the land. In the Chelmer valley the earliest tools found date from about 240,000 BC. As woolly mammoths became extinct about 1700 BC, they would have been very familiar to our hardy early ancestors, who would have pursued animals in bogs and dug pits in the approach of wandering herds, trapping the ungainly beasts and hunting them down with their primitive weapons.

Hunting a woolly mammoth in the tundra of early Essex. (Courtesy of the Museum of London)

AD **43**

ROMAN ARMIES
IN CAESAR'S FIELD

THE ROMANS HAD their own name for Chelmsford: Caesaromagus, or 'Caesar's Field'. Historians are divided on the meaning: it could denote the place where Caesar defeated the 'British' army when he seized Colchester. Alternatively, some argue for a translation of 'Caesar's Market', which is much less exciting.

Older names for the river Chelmer include 'beadu', 'baedwe' or 'badw', which means 'battle' or 'war'. Was it the Battle River? There are connections to the word in both Germanic and Old Norse languages, with possible echoes to 'holy river' or even 'war goddess' (though these are uncertain). Both Great and Little Baddow owe their names to the ancient river.

Could it be that these names remember some far-off battle, like that of Romans fighting their way from London to Colchester in AD 43? No archaeological proof has yet been found – though the legions would have passed this way to reach Colchester along the road they called Ealdan stræte.

Seventeen or eighteen years later, the local Trinovantes joined Boudicca, Queen of the Iceni, in her bloody AD 60-61 revolt against the Romans. They began with the ransacking, torching, looting and massacring of Romans and sympathisers at Colchester, where the last survivors fled to the safety of the Claudian temple and perished. The remains of that temple became the base of Colchester Castle. Boudicca and the Trinovantes marched on to London and then Verulamium (St Albans), swelling the rebel army to 100,000 men, women and children before her final defeat, when England's fiery red-haired defender took poison.

Boudicca was responsible for some 7,000 deaths, as official figures by the Roman Tacitus suggest. At Chelmsford at that time there would have been little opportunity for sacking, but she would have pushed her blood-thirsty revenge this way ...

In the aftermath, as Rome secured its hold on this far-flung island, a fort was built on the road between London and

Caesar's armies landing in Britain.

SKELETAL SHAMANS AT MOULSHAM STREET?

Chelmsford's Roman cemeteries would have been placed outside the Roman town along the road to the south. A stone coffin was discovered and rescued in 1987 in Godfrey Mews, Moulsham Street, when contractors' heavy machinery uncovered it by chance. It was an interesting find dating from the third or fourth century, and obviously of an important personage – but he or she was not alone. Nearby was found 'the skeleton of a partially burnt body', buried with a jet bracelet and a lathe-turned rod – possibly a wand of office. Jet was perceived as having magical properties – it becomes electrically charged when rubbed and it was believed that it could be ignited by water and quenched by oil.

Did a shaman or priest, half burnt on a funeral pyre, join the important person on his/her final journey?

Roman stone coffin and its occupant, at the archaeological excavation in Godfrey Mews, Moulsham Street. (Picture courtesy of Chelmford Museum)

Colchester, commanding the strategic river crossing, about a day's march from either Roman town. At first this was protected by a wooden palisade, but it was later reinforced with an earth rampart and ditch. The Chelmsford garrison, with possibly a smaller enclosure for cavalry, did not last long. It became the first road station on the route from London to Carlisle on the Wall.

Caesaromagus lay to the west of the road crossing over the Rivers Can and Chelmer, beneath modern Chelmsford in the Moulsham area, roughly defined by

Roman standards. (With kind permission of Thomas Fisher Rare Book Library, University of Toronto)

Moulsham Street, Hall Street, Hamlet Road and Mildmay Road. Beneath the Odeon roundabout lie the ruins of an octagonal temple. It would have functioned as a mansio, a road station or staging post with a villa dedicated to the travellers' rest and refreshment, the likes of which were dotted along Roman roads at regular intervals all over their Empire, usually a day's march apart. The Chelmsford version dated to around AD 120, and included a bath-house – a circular *laconicum*, a kind of sauna. A tessellated pavement discovered in the nineteenth century may have belonged to this.

The buildings were occupied until the fourth century, after which the settlement seems to have been largely abandoned. The defences were levelled during the first quarter of the third century.

The Romans left Britain as the Empire downsized, and by around AD 410 they had gone. Immigration to Britain, however, did not stop. Angles and Saxons arrived, fought and pushed the original Celts westward, settled and put their stamp on the land.

SAXON TOMBS

KINGDOMS WERE RATHER smaller in the Dark Ages, more like princely fiefdoms. Leaders were expected to reward bravery and loyalty generously. They also expressed their wealth and position by the gifts they could afford to take with them to the grave. (Contrary to the modern idiom, they could and would take it with them ...)

Some of the deceased's favourite things, they thought, would serve him well in the next world. Only the best would do – swords, intricate gold and garnet jewellery, glass and pottery. They also buried food and drink, blankets and clothes, belts and shoes – and weapons galore. At Sutton Hoo one chief even took his horse with him ...

Such a Saxon burial was accidentally discovered in 1888, in a gravel pit behind Clobb's Row, Broomfield, when workmen found remains of a sword, spear and knife 6-7ft down while digging gravel. 'A tape-like material' bound the sword's wooden sheath, and of a spear only the spearhead survived. A shield boss would once have stood proud at the centre of a wooden shield. More ostentatious, perhaps, were the finds of a gold pyramid and buckle plate, both set with garnets. A bronze pan, and reddish tufts from a 'hairy cloak' were also found. Even inclement weather was obviously catered for in the afterlife. Curiously, the grave walls were covered with soot or charcoal, and there were fragments of wood, parts of flat iron bars, angle irons and rivets from a coffin – but no body. That had been incinerated within the tomb before the grave goods were added. The finds were dated AD 600-700 and have been deposited at the British Museum. Only personages of the highest ranks would have had access to such items.

HEROES AND MAN-DEVOURING MONSTERS

Legendary poem *Beowulf* was composed in England, possibly in the early eighth century. It survives in a single fire-singed manuscript from around AD 1000.

In it, monster-slayer Beowulf is cremated on a grand funeral pyre adorned with shields and helmets. His ashes are afterwards placed in a tumulus, under a mount, together with suitable grave goods, just like our hero at Broomfield.

> The treasure of heroes they let
> the earth hold,
> gold in the gritty soil,
> where it now still lives,
> as useless to men
> as it was before.
> (Translation: Benjamin Slade)

THE BIRTH OF CHELMSFORD

CHELMSFORD'S NAME IS derived from 'Ceolmaer's ford', which was a site close to the present High Street stone bridge. Who Ceolmaer was has been lost in time, but he gave his name to both the town and the river as it meanders towards the eastern sea. The Domesday Book of 1086 names the town 'Celmeresfort'. There were many derivations, though 100 years later, by 1189, it had settled on 'Chelmsford'. Moulsham was Mulesham and Molesham in 1066, remembering 'Mul's farm'.

At the time of the Norman Conquest of 1066, Chelmsford, on the northern side of the Can, belonged to Bishop William of London, where it remained under the new order. The river Can was the border between the lands of two religious owners: the Moulsham side remained in the hands of the Abbot of St Peter's, Westminster. Chelmsford was but a small settlement with four villagers or households after the conquest – there had been five before. There was a mill and woodland enough for 300 pigs.

After 1066, the old Saxon hierarchy had been swept away and largely replaced by Normans who arrived with the Conqueror. From that time the king owned everything, but he graciously handed estates out to his friends and supporters. They, in turn, were paid by the lower classes in money or more likely in service. Freemen could farm their land or carry out a business, but serfs were beholden to the Manor as villans (villains or *villeins*), bordars and lowest of all, slaves.

Westminster's Moulsham Lodge had been reduced from eight villagers before the Conquest to three villagers after, but the number of smallholders had grown from four to twenty-one. One mill was registered and there was woodland for 400 pigs.

Moulsham Halls (in the north of the hundred) had been taken from a Saxon called Godric and another called Wolfmer. Both manors were in the hands of Bishop William now. Villagers and smallholders had increased from two to eight, but slaves had been reduced from four to three in one of them. Wulfmer's plot still had one smallholder and two slaves. Between them the hall manors included woodland for 100 pigs. As well as slaves, in 1086 there was still a considerable acreage of the old Essex forest left.

By far the greater communities in the hundred of Chelmsford were Writtle, with some 175 males and (Great and Little) Waltham with 154. (The Domesday Book survey did not bother with women and children.) Writtle had belonged to King Harold before 1066 – the Crown having taken Robert the Bruce's estates – now it was held directly by King William. There was enough woodland to support 1200 pigs, and there were two mills. Writtle also paid the highest taxes.

Ceolmaer's Ford and Horsepond, the original Roman site of the ford, as it was painted by Donald Maxwell in 1925. The original sixteenth-century bridge was removed in 1960. With due regard to the historic origins of Chelmsford it has been replaced with the Springfield Road roundabout at High Bridge Road and Bond Street. It used to be part of the historic Mesopotamia Island. (Maxwell, D., Unknown Essex, 1925)

The northern side of the Can was owned by the more active of the two religious houses. In about the year 1100 Bishop Maurice had bridges rebuilt over the rivers Can and Chelmer, a sound commercial venture resulting in the re-direction of traffic from Writtle to the old Roman road through Chelmsford along Moulsham Street.

The former fording place on the river Can at Ceolmaer's Ford was a natural site for trade. In 1199 the overlord was Bishop William of Sainte-Mère-Eglise. The Norman was granted a Royal Charter by King John with the right to hold a weekly market near the bridge. This was followed in 1201 with the right to hold an annual fair in Chelmsford, also not necessarily for altruistic reasons. The Bishop held the prebend of Ealdstreet, i.e. the revenues, among his portfolio. When King Richard I was captured in Sicily on his return from the Third Crusade, it was this Bishop William, together with Hubert Walter, bishop of

The Shire Hall is just the latest version of the Court buildings where justice has been dispensed almost since the beginnings of Chelmsford, which became the seat of the local Assize early in the thirteenth century. The market was held in the foreground.

Salisbury, who found the King where he was being held captive at Ochsenfurt in Germany. William of Sainte-Mère-Eglise was the guardian of the amounts due to be collected for Richard's ransom in the south of England, a story well known from the exploits of Robin Hood.

The bishop's local innovations were the beginning of the growth of the modern town of Chelmsford. An under-cover market is still an important part of the town centre more than 800 years later. The central position in Essex, in addition, fostered the establishment as the County Town with the Assizes.

Sometime before 1277 a Dominican Friary (Black Friars) was founded here in the vicinity of what is now Friar's Walk. The Dominican order has produced many prominent theologians since their founding in 1216. Archaeological excavations in the 1960s and '70s established the former sites of the dorter undercroft, parts of the north range, reredorter, cloister walk and north-east corner of the chapter house. Also, in the late thirteenth century a leper hostel was established at Moulsham.

The Friary was dissolved again in Henry VIII's purge of 1538. Where once learned monks walked the floor of the chapter house, the new order after the plunder of the Dissolution of Monasteries saw fit to replace their legacy with a more down-to-earth lime kiln. Another result of the Dissolution was the closure of many hospitals and the dispersal of the monks and/or nuns that had attended the sick and ailing.

Moulsham, while remaining a distinct and separate hamlet, became the poor relation to go-ahead Chelmsford, later receiving a gaol and a workhouse.

In its position on a main road, medieval Chelmsford prospered. A leather industry developed with skinners and tanners, as well as a wool industry with weavers and fullers and drapers and mercers, the dealers in fine cloth.

ROBERT THE BRUCE IN CHELMSFORD

WAS ROBERT THE Bruce, the epic hero of Scotland, actually born at Montpeliers Farm, Writtle, near Chelmsford? The place of his birth is disputed, but probable. There certainly was a close connection between the Bruce family and Essex at the time.

His father, Sir Robert de Brus, 6th Lord of Annandale, Earl of Carrick, Lord of Hartness, Writtle and Hatfield Broad Oak was a cross-border lord with estates both in Scotland and Essex. When he married Marjorie of Carrick he added that estate to his own.

Their son, Robert, was born on 11 July 1274. King Edward I (Longshanks) returned from the Ninth Crusade to England on 2 August that year, to be crowned King. On 19 August the Bruces attended the Coronation and accompanying celebrations of Edward I at Westminster, together with Alexander III of Scots, his Queen Margaret, their children and '100 Scottish lords and knights'. The question of a Writtle birth for the man who was to become King of the Scots rests on these dates: would the young couple have travelled from Scotland to attend the Coronation, or would – given his wife's recent confinement – the pair have come from nearby Writtle? The second seems more likely.

We can trace Bruce senior to Writtle again on 1 January 1293, when he had to deal with his warrener Richard at Great Baddow, who – maybe tired of rabbit stew – had been caught poaching venison. He was

King Edward I (Longshanks), the hated Hammer of the Scots.

Robert the Bruce, proud on his plinth near Stirling.

in Essex many times, though his stays were interrupted by wars in which he fought beside Edward I.

Robert de Bruce senior died at Easter 1304, en route to Annandale, and lies buried at Holm Cultram Abbey, Cumberland. His son, Robert the Bruce, was inaugurated as King of Scots at Scone Abbey, Perthshire, on 27 March 1306.

Being related to or marrying into the Bruce family would be a life-shortening experience if caught by Edward I or his friends, certainly for the male line.

�֍ Countess Isobel of Fife was held captive in an iron cage that hung over the walls of Berwick Castle.

✖ Robert's younger sister, Mary Bruce, was locked into an iron cage at Roxburgh Castle. She was just twenty-four years of age, but she spent the next four years caged and humiliated.

✖ Another sister, Christian Bruce, was shown more compassion. She was imprisoned in a Gilbertine nunnery in Lincolnshire.

✖ Her husband, Sir Christopher Seton, was hanged, drawn and beheaded at Dumfries.

✖ Robert's daughter Marjorie was only twelve years old when she was captured at Tain. King Edward considered locking her into an iron cage to be hung from the walls of the Tower of London as a spectacle, but he relented. The child was sent to a Gilbertine nunnery in Yorkshire.

✖ Elizabeth de Burgh, Bruce's wife, was kept prisoner in England. For eight years she was moved from place to place.

✖ Neil (Niall or Nigel) de Bruce was taken prisoner at Kildrummie, and hanged, drawn and beheaded at Berwick-upon-Tweed in September 1306.

✖ Brothers Sir Thomas and Alexander de Brus were taken prisoner in Galloway, and both hanged, drawn and quartered on 9 February 1307 at Carlisle, Cumberland.

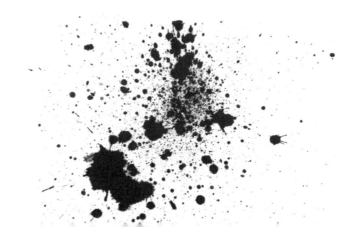

AD 1349

THE BLACK DEATH STRIKES!

BROUGHT IN ON ships from Asia, the Black Death or Bubonic Plague, foraging east, arrived in Essex in the spring of 1349. That very year the abbot's bailiff in Moulsham recorded the sad statement that there were no rents from thirty-one tenements because tenants were dead, and that necessary work (such as hoeing) had to be abandoned for lack of labour. Thirty-one households destroyed in Moulsham alone!

There is no comparable record for the town-dwellers over the stream in Chelmsford, but Lynches – an upland holding 'in decay for want of a tenant with buildings falling in' – was vacant in 1383 and had been in the lord's hands since 'the first pestilence'. That would suggest that – bad as the first outbreak was – the locality did not escape the later outbreaks of 1361-2 and 1369 either.

The bacterial disease spread rapidly, especially in towns and cities, transferred from black rats to humans – and then from human to human – by the rat flea. A bite by an infected flea was followed by a painful infection that could take just a few days – usually three to four – to kill a human. Few recovered. Massive swelling and infection of the lymph nodes are typical signs, especially in the armpit and groin, which ooze pus and blood. Such blackened areas of swelling were called 'buboes'. They gave the bubonic plague its name (though there were also two other forms of the Black Death).

A total of 1.5 million people – of an estimated total of 4 million people – are thought to have died in England between 1348 and 1350. After 1350, the plague was to strike England another six times by the end of the century. Medical knowledge was practically non-existent to cope with the disease, and cleanliness was no priority in the Dark Ages either. We may gain some insight into sanitary conditions in Chelmsford during those dark times from the fact that in 1475 – when most people kept pigs – the townsfolk were forbidden to let their pigs roam the streets!

One consequence of so many people dying, with whole families and villages wiped out, was that fields remained unploughed and unharvested, and animals were left untended or lost. Whole neighbourhoods therefore faced starvation.

A close look at the culprit who spread death across Britain and Europe, the infecting flea! (Janice Haney Carr, PD-USGov-HHS-CDC)

The battle between good and evil, as seen when the pestilence threatened to wipe out humanity.

There was, however, an upside to all this horror: those remaining felt they were 'chosen to survive', and a new self-worth permeated the communities. Surviving labourers felt empowered to demand higher wages – or they would move to where the pay was better. This could not be allowed. In an attempt to keep wages at the pre-plague level and so perpetuate the *status quo* of feudalism, Edward III's Parliament, composed almost entirely of landowners, passed the Statute of Labourers in 1351, litigating 'against the malice of servants which were idle and not willing to serve after the pestilence without taking excessive wages'. The Act demanded that:

✕ 'Every person able in body under the age of sixty years ... shall be bound to serve him that doth require him, or else be committed to gaol ...'

✕ 'If a workman or servant depart from service before the time agreed he shall be imprisoned.'
✕ 'The old wages and no more shall be given to servants.'
✕ 'If any ... take more wages than were wont to be paid he shall be committed to gaol.'
✕ 'Victuals shall be sold at reasonable prices.'

The Act was Parliament's attempt to freeze wages and so stop employers paying over the odds to secure much needed workers. The penalty for such employers was heavy fines. However, this Act had quite the opposite effect to the one intended: rather than ensure the status quo, it laid the foundation for a revolt.

The Act was also difficult to enforce. It had to be re-enacted in 1357 and 1360, each time with more severe penalties. However, it was obviously not working, for in 1351 no less than seventy-seven employers in Chelmsford and Moulsham were penalised. Usually these fines were between 2 shillings and a mark (about 13 shillings and 4 pence). However, in Chelmsford and Moulsham the fines amounted to a lot more:

✕ £25 7s 4d at Chelmsford and Moulsham
✕ £8 2s 4d at Writtle
✕ £5 11s at Great Baddow
✕ 30s at Springfield
✕ 21s 8d at Broomfield
✕ One Chelmsford employer, William of Birchanger, of an unidentified business, was fined no less than a colossal £100, a sum unequalled in Essex.

Had Chelmsford's realistic stance in the labour market been adopted nationally, the peasants' uprising of 1381 might never have happened.

A BRIDGE TOO FAR?

We may find possible evidence of this renewed power of the common tradesman and artisan in the cost of building a new bridge in Chelmsford in 1360-61.

This era marked the beginning of the Hundred Years' War – for which Chelmsford supplied one armed foot soldier, John Porter, and several archers – and was a time when Chelmsford and Moulsham had their own differences.

As a natural halting place in journeys between London and the coast of Essex and East Anglia, for both rich and poor folk alike, the traffic generated over the past 250 years had not been kind to the old bridge of 'Celmeresford'. But just who was responsible for the upkeep of the bridge? Both sides insisted their half – to midstream – was in good repair. The battle of the bridges was about to begin!

- ✳ Firstly, two carpenters were hired to repair the bridge at a cost of no more than 8 pence.
- ✳ A second repair was made in 1360-1, which cost a hefty £6 9s 6d – though that included a fine of 3s 4d for not doing it properly in the first place!

A report was then made, in 1360-1, which suggested that the bridge (which was made of wood) was in a dire state: the carriageway underfoot was collapsing. To address this was an expensive undertaking:

- ✳ A carpenter was hired to repair it at £3 6s 8d.
- ✳ He was supported by two sawyers, each paid 5 pence a day for eighteen days.
- ✳ Eight extra men (paid 3 pence each for eight days) were hired to lift old timbers and relay new ones.
- ✳ Carters were hired, who each commanded 1 shilling per day. Five of these carters collected timber from Feering; one spent five days carrying timber cut in Moulsham, while another spent three days carrying hurdles to the bridge. Two others carried gravel.
- ✳ The miller at the Earl of Hereford's Mill at Writtle was paid 4 shillings to hold back the water at the mill, so the water level was low enough for work on the bridge to be carried out. (This was possible, as the mill stood at the junction of the Can, Wid and Roxwell Brook.)

None of these were the going rates at the time – Chelmsford's workers had successfully demanded a higher wage for their work.

FLAGELLANTS – REDEMPTION THROUGH PAIN

Plague seemed to strike at random. With the lack of understanding of its causes and the actual way it spread, theories abounded. Was it bred in the overheated excitement of crowds, as in a theatre? Did it travel in foul air? Was it God's way of punishing mankind?

Religious leaders thought it was. Extreme expressions of human repentance appeared across the lands, and groups of itinerant flagellants sought redemption and survival though self-chastisement. The more it hurt, they thought, the more likely God would be to listen. Fears and anxieties spread, breeding suspicions and feeding beliefs in black magic and witchcraft. Was the plague in fact the beginning of the Apocalypse? Flagellants across the country sought to guarantee their place in the coming afterlife – with blood.

THE ROBBER AND THE HANGMAN

'Ten or twelve on a beam... because they were too
many to be executed after the usual manner...'

Judge Tresilian's Bloody Assizes of 1381

THE YEAR WAS 1381.
Following the many deaths from the plague, and in the wake of Edward III's many treasury-draining wars, poll taxes had been introduced, one in 1377 and another one in 1379. Those had been onerous enough, but in 1381 a third poll-tax was demanded: 4 groats (1 shilling 4 pence) per adult over fifteen years of age.

When the last treasurer, Bishop Brantingham of Exeter, resigned, Sir Robert Hales, Prior of the Knights Hospitallers, was appointed in his place; the labourers called him 'Hobbe the Robber'. He was to become the most hated man in England.

The spark which set the powder keg aflame was lit in Fobbing in Essex on the 30 May, when Hobbe's poll-tax collectors, arriving to collect this third tax, were sent packing with nothing. Robert Belknap, the Chief Justice of the Court of Common Pleas, was sent to punish the defaulting villagers. As soon as he reached Brentwood, he was attacked.

Rebellion spread like wildfire. For a brief space of time, the peasant classes tasted freedom: they left their shovels and hovels, and banded together to march on London. Their grievances were many, but they could not turn to Parliament, which consisted mainly of landowners who had instigated the 'Statute of Labourers' Act of 1351. Instead, they sought to speak to the King. Along the way they burnt any documents they could find, along with any parchment scrolls (which were seen as the shackles of their servitude) – and sometimes they burnt down the houses where they found them too. At Cressing Temple, the house of 'Hobbe the Robber' was attacked and sacked.

Admittedly, some hotheads went too far: several landlords and officials were beheaded by the mob, and many houses were plundered when the papers were destroyed. The rioters felt that they were only taking back what had been taken from them. There were so many of them then ...

When the peasant army reached London and met the King, the young Richard II, he promised that he would deal with his officials, and grant rioters safe conduct and immunity from prosecution.

He lied.

A royal army was assembled, and the uprising in the shires was brutally dealt with. On 22 June, the King set off at the head of an army. The next day they reached Waltham, from where Richard issued a proclamation that set the tone for what was to come. He had not, he stated, and never did have any sympathy for those who broke the law and acted against Crown and Kingdom with their riotous and treasonable conduct. The pledges made on June 14 and 15 counted for nothing, as they had been made under duress. They could tear up the promises he'd made:

'Villeins ye are still, and villeins ye shall remain!' he is said to have proclaimed.

Generally speaking, there had been few troubles in Chelmsford – though the Sheriff of Essex was threatened and assaulted by rebellious peasants during the unrest, and 'all writs of green wax' were burnt.

Richard II and his court are thought to have stayed at Writtle. They reached Chelmsford on 2 July, revoking all charters, pledges and promises made during the uprising. There would be no amnesty either. A judicial inquiry would be set up, with powers to look into all the actions of the rebels from the first days of the insurgency. With the King and his court officiating, and despatching orders, deeds and declarations to all parts of the Kingdom, for a short time Chelmsford was – to all intents and purposes – the capital of England.

Punishment was swift.

> Essex men, in a body of about 500, addressed themselves barefoot to the King for mercy, and had it granted upon condition that they should deliver up to justice the chief instruments of stirring up the rebellion; which being accordingly done, they were immediately tried and hanged, ten or twelve on a beam, at Chelmsford, because they were too many to be executed after the usual manner, which was by beheading.

The judgement of Robert Tresilian seems to permeate that account. Ten Fobbing men were condemned at Chelmsford in July 1381. At least five were hanged. Thomas Baker of Fobbing, the first identified rebel, was drawn and hanged on 4 July.

Men from South Benfleet, Leigh, Hadleigh, Bowers Gifford, Rayleigh, Rawreth and Fobbing had joined in the attack of the Manor of Barnhall at Downham on 12 June. They, too, were tried

A 'pious' Richard II being presented to the Madonna and Child by his patron saint John the Baptist with kings Edward the Confessor and Edmund the Martyr from the Wilton diptych. (With kind permission of Thomas Fisher Rare Book Library, University of Toronto)

before Judge Tresilian at Chelmsford.

The commissioners Robert Tresilian and William Morrers sat at Havering and then Chelmsford, but it was Robert Tresilian whose name was to spread fear throughout the realm. A document from the time names the jurors, who:

> ... say upon their oaths that William ate Stable, late servant of Geoffrey Dersham, Thomas Sprag (Spraggle) of South Benfleet, Richard Bertram, herdsman in South Benfleet Marsh, Robert Maryn of South Benfleet, Nichola Cartere who was lately taken as wife by William Dekne of South Benfleet, Thomas Treche de la Leye, William Bocher of Hadley, John Colyn of Hadley, wright, and his two sons, William Bocher of Hadley, Richard Belle

DEATH OF THE NAKED JUDGE

In November 1386, Parliament appointed a commission to review and control royal finances. The King resented that infringement of his Royal prerogative, and Tresilian drafted a document that turned the tables on Parliament.

The King's opponents went on the counterattack, and on 17 November 1387 Tresilian was among a number of loyalists who were charged with treason by the group of noblemen known as the Lords Appellant. It came to an armed confrontation – and the Lords won. When Tresilian's case came up for trial, however, he had gone into hiding and was sentenced *in absentia*. Not long afterwards he was discovered close to Parliament, disguised as an old man and 'looking more like a pilgrim or beggar than a King's justice…'.

Others accused with him had fled abroad, where they lived out their lives, but Tresilian was the most sought after. With the cry: 'We havet hym! We havet hym!', he was taken to Parliament. In the presence of his wife and children he was tied to a hurdle, and accompanied by 'a vast multitude' of lords and commoners, horsemen and pedestrians, he was drawn through the city from the back of horses.

And when he had come to the place of Calvary that he might be made defunct, he did not want to climb the stairs but goaded by sticks and whips that he might ascend, he said, 'While I carry a certain something around me, I am not able to die.' Immediately they stripped him and found particular instructions with particular signs depicted in them, in the manner of astronomical characters; and one depicted a demon's head, many others were inscribed with demons' names. With these taken away, he was hanged nude, and for greater certainty of his death his throat was cut.

Had the merciless judge made a pact with the Devil? If so, it was not enough to save him …

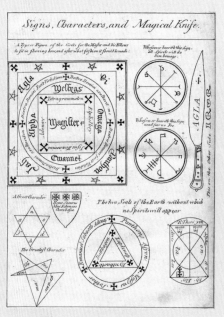

When it came to his own final moments, Judge Robert Tresilian's magical symbols were unable to save him: 'whoever beareth this sign,' the writer claimed, 'need fear no Foe' – unless it is discovered on the gallows, that is! (www.fromoldbooks.org)

of Hadley, John Symond of Hadley, Peter Pekok of Bures Giffard, John ate Merssh of Hadley and Henry Fleccher of Ralegh, on the Wednesday next after the Feast of Trinity in the fourth year of King Richard II led and supported the commons to the manor of Geoffrey Dersham of Bernhalle [Barnhall?] and feloniously and traitorously stole and carried off 5 cows priced at 5 marks, 3 calves priced at 20 shillings, 140 sheep priced at £16, and pots and pans and other goods and chattels of the same Geoffrey worth 60 shillings; and furthermore broke and levelled the house of the same Geoffrey and feloniously took and carried away 120 chickens priced at 40 shillings.

And furthermore they all rode armed through the peaceful countryside raising the aforesaid commons against the King and his laws to the Temple of the Priory of St John in England at Cressy and to the house of John Sewale of Coggeshalle, and they levelled the houses of the aforesaid Prior and John and feloniously came upon and took away their goods and chattels. Moreover, they say that on Friday next after the Feast of the Holy Trinity in the fourth year of the reign of the aforesaid King Richard II, John Wiltshire of Lesser Burstede freely and without compulsion lopped off the head of a certain esquire of the Duke of Lancaster called Grenefeld in the City of London.

Nineteen men were hanged, while another twelve were hanged, drawn and quartered.

There is one woman listed among the accused. We don't know what happened to her. Perhaps Nichola Carter, new wife of William Dekne of South Benfleet, was able to claim pregnancy and so escape her fate?

One source says of Tresilian and his 'Bloody Assize': 'He pressured jurors into giving up names of suspects, and to maximise sentences, contrived to have charges presented as Felony rather than Trespass.'

By the 14 July Tresilian had moved on to St Albans, where he tried and sentenced the Priest John Ball, among others. In all, it is reckoned he sentenced to death some 500 rebels.

BLOODY MARY

WITH ITS FINE Tudor façade, New Hall's main building is magnificent: Grade I listed, its heritage setting includes a historic avenue of trees, and a Grade II registered park and garden. Only the north wing of a once much larger palace has survived.

In 1062, four years before the Norman Conquest, the manor of Walhfare in Boreham was granted to the canons of Waltham Abbey. Various changes of ownership later, in 1491, it was in the hands of the Earl of Ormond, including a 'New Hall'. By 1516, New Hall belonged to Thomas Bullen (later Boleyn), who sold it to Henry VIII for £1,000. The young King had great plans for what he was to call his Palace of Beaulieu, 'the beautiful place'.

Arms of Henry VIII as they survive in New Hall's chapel.

He was in probably the most exalted stage of his life and had it rebuilt in brick and extended at a remarkable cost of £17,000, an elaborate and worthy home for his firstborn, and ordered just a month before her birth. Alas, the firstborn was a girl – Princess Mary (later called 'Bloody Mary', because history is written by the victors). Catherine of Aragon had other children, but none survived.

The palace was huge, having eight courtyards with a 550ft-wide façade. Two massive gatehouse towers added to the impressive splendour. Built in the latest fashion, based on a series of perfect squares, Beaulieu incorporated architectural ideas imported from Rome. This was discovered by archaeology nearly 500 years later when Channel Four's *Time Team* dug up the foundations in February 2009. The excavations uncovered the chapel, the west wing and the gatehouse. But there was another surprise: an 'intricate series of Tudor drains where the western range would have stood' suggested a second kitchen or laundry area. It could only have been intended for a nursery, indicating the young King's preparation for an expected birth. Beaulieu would be a statement of grandeur, though he had inherited several palaces from his father and was to build many more. The royal inventory of 1547 noted twenty-nine great beds, four bathing rooms with wooden floors and beds set in

Beaulieu Palace as it would have appeared in around 1580, worthy of a young king with high hopes. Only the part at top right (opposite the towers) survives as today's school. (Image reproduced courtesy of New Hall School – www.newhallschool.co.uk)

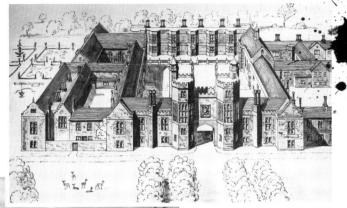

New Hall today, still grand, but a small survivor of Beaulieu's former glory. What whispers these walls could tell; what joy they saw and what tears ...

the wall, and a library with thirty-seven books.

On 23 July 1527, Henry's court arrived at Beaulieu on his summer progress in the company of a great many nobles and their wives, including: Anne Boleyn's father, Thomas Boleyn; Viscount Fitzwalter; the earls of Oxford, Essex and Rutland; the marquess of Exeter; and the dukes of Norfolk and Suffolk. They stayed far longer than usual, for Anne joined Henry at Beaulieu in August that year and spent the greater part of a month there, enjoying their favourite pastimes: hunting and hawking by day, music, poetry, dancing, cards, dice – and whatever lovers do, supping each evening in his privy chamber. It is thought to have been here that Henry concocted a scheme to allow him to cohabit with Anne.

By 1531, the King's pleasures were changing. Christmas 1531 was spent at Greenwich without Queen Catherine and without Princess Mary, who now spent her time isolated at Beaulieu. All contact between mother and daughter was forbidden; her parents' marriage was annulled, her place in succession was cancelled and she was referred to only as 'Lady Mary'. When her half-sister Elizabeth was born, her father severed all ties with her. In October 1533, Mary was evicted and the palace granted to Anne Boleyn's brother George, who had formerly been a keeper at Beaulieu on behalf of the King. Mary became a lowly lady-in-waiting in her half-sister's household.

Less than three years later, however, both Anne and her brother were beheaded. In the 'Second Act of Succession' in 1536, Parliament declared both Elizabeth and the nineteen-year-old Mary illegitimate. Her position was now desperate.

Luckily, however, Mary's half-brother Edward handed the magnificent building to her 'for life'. The first-born daughter

Above, left and centre: *The famous Hollar sketches of Henry VIII and Anne Boleyn, who plotted their union at Beaulieu. (With kind permission of Thomas Fisher Rare Book Library, University of Toronto)*

Right: *Queen Mary I spent a miserable youth at Beaulieu from 1532. Soon after that she was declared a royal bastard ...*

of the King and his Catholic first Queen, Mary became a rallying point for Catholics; this put her life in grave danger – threats to the Crown were not tolerated. On several occasions loyal followers moved her secretly from Beaulieu to a safe house owned by the Fitzwalters at Woodham Walter, and a boat was kept in readiness at Maldon in case she had to be smuggled to the Continent. When she at last gained the throne of England, her reign was a short and 'bloody' one.

Illustrious owners would follow. After Mary's death in 1558, possibly from uterine cancer, Queen Elizabeth I granted the Beaulieu estate to Thomas Radcliffe, 3rd Earl of Sussex in 1573. Much rebuilding was necessary – there had been a fire in Henry VIII's time – and certainly the north wing was largely rebuilt. Then, in 1622,

George Villiers, 1st Duke of Buckingham, purchased the estate for £30,000. Oliver Cromwell afterwards acquired it for the grand sum of 5 shillings during the Civil War in 1640. At the Restoration it reverted back to the 2nd Duke of Buckingham and was sold to George Monck, 1st Duke of Albermarle, who frequently entertained Charles II's court here; even Charles II's and the people's favourite Nell Gwyn – 'pretty, witty Nell' – dined here.

Ironically, perhaps, what was left of Henry VIII's palace was acquired in 1798 by the English nuns of the Order of the Holy Sepulchre, who opened a Catholic school here the following year. It's known as New Hall again, and a school still. Henry VIII's original Arms survive in the school chapel. The Beaulieu name is remembered in a nearby housing estate, Beaulieu Park.

AD **1430–1582**

THE TERRIFYING TRUE STORY OF TRUDGEOVER EAGLE

THE BURNING OF WILLIAM CALEYS AND THE HERETICAL DOCTRINE OF THE LOLLARDS

Even today there are still fanatics who believe it is your lot to die if you don't believe what they believe. In medieval England that was a policy backed and enforced by law. The 'Lollards' were a network of 'heretics', more than 100 of which could be found in the Norfolk-Suffolk border area in the 1420s. They believed:

✗ That baptism was unnecessary
✗ That confessions ought to be made only to God
✗ That no one should get married in church ('a simple agreement between man and woman to love one another is sufficient')
✗ That swearing an oath was unlawful
✗ That physical activity, excepting sinful, was acceptable on Sundays
✗ That all tithes should be withheld from curates and priests and given to the poor
✗ That there should be no obligation to fast at Lent or Fridays

The seeds of Puritanism are inherent in those doctrines and notions, many of which have since been adopted by law, but in 1428 one case in Colchester elicited a writ from King Henry VI to the town's bailiffs, demanding that such a heretic should be 'burned in fiery flames'.

Henry wrote:

We order you as firmly as we can that the aforesaid William, who is now in your custody, be placed in the fire in some open and public location within the liberty of the town, the reason for the proceeding having been announced to the populace; and that he in that fire be burned. This you are to have done as a clear example to other Christians of how abhorrent is this kind of crime. Should you fail to carry this out in any regard, it will be at your peril. Witnessed by myself, at Westminster, 2 November 1428.

William Chivelyng was burnt in Colchester on 4 November 1428.

Another William, William Caleys, a priest with a connection to the Colchester Lollards, was burnt 'in fiery flames' at Chelmsford in 1430. No mercy was to be granted, and no repentance recognised.

THOMAS WATTS' FIERY END

In Britain's past, not worshipping in a certain fashion was made a criminal offence: treason. Executions varied: sometimes burning to death was the preferred option, and at other times it was hanging, drawing and quartering.

'The burning of Thomas Wattes, Martyr', from 'Actes and Monuments...' by John Foxe. (1563-1583). John Wattes calmly reassures his friends before his fiery demise. (The Unabridged Acts and Monuments Online (HRI Online Publications, Sheffield, 2011).

Chelmsford, as seat of the County Assises, has its own ample examples. In 1555, a letter was sent by exasperated Essex justices to Bishop Bonner of London. The gentlemen of the law could not deal with the arguments of the man in their charge, so they wanted to pass him on. The letter concludes:

> ... certifying you further, that in our opinion he is one of the most arrogant heretics that hath been heard speak, or ever came before you, and not meet (suitable) to be kept here in any gaol, as well for fear of corrupting others, as for divers and sundry other special causes hereafter to be more declared. Thus leaving to molest your good Lordship, we commit you to the Holy Ghost.
>
> Given at Chelmsford the twenty-seventh of April, Anno 1555. Your good Lordship's most assured: R. Riche, Henry Tyrrel, Anthony Brown, Edmund Tyrrel, Thomas Mildmay, John Wiseman, Roger Appleton, Richard Weston.

The man in question was Thomas Watts, a linen draper from Billericay. Watts was accused of not coming to church. He pointed out that the justice who sentenced him, Justice Anthony Brown, had previously condemned prisoners for *not* sharing Watts' views, but it made no difference. Bishop Bonner could not change the mind of the draper either, though he was examined on several occasions. Thomas Watts was condemned. He returned to Chelmsford, where he was taken to Scot's house, 'keeping then an inn in Chelmsford', where he met with other believers, all sentenced to die at various places throughout Essex. Scot's house was in the High Street, by the bridge over the river Can.

According to *Foxe's Book of Martyrs*, when Watts said goodbye to his wife and six children two of them offered to join him in the flames. And so he was carried to the fire under the odious Lord Rich, who had helped to condemn people under two previous monarchs, and would slaughter more men under the next. Watts is said to have warned Lord Rich – after kissing the stake and before he was burnt near the Shire Hall – on the 10 June 1555:

> 'My Lord,' saith he, 'beware, beware! For you do against your own conscience herein; and without you repent, the Lord will revenge it: for you are the cause of this, my death.'

TRUDGEOVER EAGLE'S TERRIBLE PASSING

George Eagles had preached during young Edward VI's reign, but then Edward's half-sister Mary came to the throne; he was one of the preachers of the Protestant faith who fell foul of Mary's spies.

A tailor by trade, he trudged from market place to market place preaching the Protestant cause. His peripatetic lifestyle earned him the nickname 'Trudge-over-the-world Eagles', which was commonly shortened to 'Trudgeover'. When he came to the attention of the Queen's advisors, a royal proclamation was sent out through Essex and neighbouring counties, offering a reward of £20 for information leading to his capture.

He was preaching in Colchester one market day – Mary Magdalene's Day, 1557 – when the authorities at last caught up with him. He managed to flee, hiding himself in a cornfield. One of his pursuers, a criminal called John Eliot, earned – and was paid – his Judas money when he betrayed Trudgeover to his terrible death: he saw the corn move as the desperate preacher wriggled away. George Eagles was caught, taken to London, accused, and sentenced to death, before being taken to Chelmsford's Crown Inn, which served as the county prison at the time. He was accused of preaching against the Queen: 'God should turn Queen Mary's heart, or else take her away,' he retorted. (He owned up to the former, but denied ever having said 'take her away'.)

The tailor suffered the full brutality of the law at Chelmsford: he was tied to a hurdle and dragged down the High Street by a horse. At the Stone Bridge a gibbet had been set up, and there he was hanged; then, before death could release him, that rope was cut.

> [He] was cut downe when he was but halfe dead, and so opened. Notwithstandinge, the blessed servaunt of Christe abode stedfast and constant in the very middest of his tormentes, till such tyme as his tormentor did plucke the hart out of the bodye. The body being divided into foure quarters, was sent abroade into foure severall places: his head was set upon a long poule at Colchestre.

Trudgeover died like that, butchered and bloody. Disembowelled, his body was cut in quarters, to be put on display in the market places of Chelmsford, Colchester, Harwich and St Osyths. Thus the severed pieces would serve as a warning to others. George 'Trudgeover' Eagles was the only Protestant of the reformation period accused of treason. He was martyred in Chelmsford.

Under 'Bloody Mary' (1553-1558), of the 300 or so 'heretics' tortured and then killed or burned at the stake, seventy-three came from Essex.

JOHN PAYNE – HANGED, DRAWN AND QUARTERED FOR HIS FAITH

Under Elizabeth I, Catholicism again came to the dock. Not adhering to the new religion was an act of treason against the state, i.e. the monarch – and that meant, in 1551, the gruesome and inhuman death that had been around since the reigns of King Henry III (1216–1272) and his successor, Edward I (1272–1307). Martyrs again faced the rope and the butcher's knife of the cruellest of all deaths: that of hanging, drawing and quartering.

There were exceptions, but over a period of several centuries many accused suffered this fate, the law's ultimate degradation. During Elizabeth's reign this included many English Catholic priests, and following the execution of King Charles I in 1649 it involved several of the regicides. In 1552 the witnesses required in accusations of treason were doubled (to two), though prisoners were presumed guilty from the outset.

The full sentence passed upon those convicted of high treason was not for the faint-hearted:

> That you be drawn on a hurdle (by a horse) to the place of execution, where you shall be hanged by the neck and being (still) alive cut down, your privy members shall be cut off and your bowels taken out and burned before you, your head severed from your body and your body divided

into four quarters to be disposed of at the King's pleasure.

Usually the remains were then despatched to be displayed in prominent, but different, places across the country. Women convicted of high treason were instead burnt at the stake – for reasons of public decency!

John Paine had been ordained as a priest at the English College of Douai in 1576. On his return to England that year he mainly worked in Essex from the home of Lady Ann Petre (widow of Sir William Petre) of Ingatestone Hall. He was betrayed and subjected to several periods on the rack in the Tower of London, from whence he was taken – at night – to be delivered to Chelmsford jail. A pettier punishment befell him first: on his sudden departure from the Tower, his purse was stolen by the Lieutenant's wife.

He was indicted at Chelmsford on 22 March, on a charge of treason, namely 'conspiring to murder the Queen and her leading officers and install Mary, Queen of Scots, on the throne'. Payne denied the charges, insisting on his loyalty to the Queen in all that was lawful (i.e. not contrary to his Catholicism or allegiance to the Pope), and questioning the reliability of the state's witness – a murderer and a rapist. However, there was to be no escape. He seems to have been resigned to his fate: 'If it please the Queen and her Council that I shall die, I refer my cause to God.'

A pardon was offered, nine months after his imprisonment, if he would recant his faith – but he refused. He was dragged from the prison on a hurdle to his place of execution. There he 'prayed on his knees for almost half an hour,' kissed the scaffold, 'made a profession of faith and declared his innocence'. Again it was Lord Rich who encouraged him to repent of his treason, which he still denied. As the execution went ahead and Payne was turned off the ladder, the crowd, it is said, had become so sympathetic that 'they hung on his feet to speed his death and prevented the infliction of the quartering until he was dead'.

John Payne was hanged, drawn and quartered at Chelmsford on 2 April 1582. He was later added to a group of Catholic martyrs, named the Forty Martyrs of England and Wales. A Roman Catholic secondary school in Chelmsford town centre is named after him.

The barbaric punishment of hanging, drawing and quartering was only finally abolished in England by the Forfeiture Act of 1870.

THE REVD THOMAS HOOKER (1586-1647) – THE ONE THAT GOT AWAY

During an outbreak of the plague in 1625, Thomas Hooker came to Chelmsford. He was to be the new lecturer and curate at St Mary's Church (now the cathedral). Educated and newly graduated from Emmanuel, the most Puritan of colleges in Cambridge University, his sermons seem to have been successful and popular. John Burles, maltster and innkeeper of the Maidenham Inn in Duke Street, was dying of the plague when he dictated his will on his sickbed on 26 August, leaving 20 shillings to Mr Hooker, 'preacher of God's word in Chelmsford'.

People flocked to his sermons on the first Friday every month, but Bishop Laud of London – in whose diocese Chelmsford then lay – did not approve of his outspoken views, and Hooker was ejected from his appointment. In 1630 he started a school for young ministers at nearby Little Baddow, in a farmhouse called Cuckoos. (It's still there.) John Eliot (no relation to the Eliot above), who later became a missionary to the Native American Indians – 'the Indian apostle' – was his assistant.

Chelmsford's Cathedral. In Thomas Hooker's days it was still St Mary's parish church.

When Hooker was forced out he moved to Lyons Hall, near Bocking, Braintree, as the tutor and resident chaplain of the Goodwin Family. With his encouragement William and Ozias Goodwin formed the Braintree Co. – recruiting others to take passage to America. A ship, *Lyon*, was chartered, and the first group sailed for New England on 2 June 1632, arriving at Boston, Massachusetts. They remembered their hometowns and villages in the names they gave their new settlements, such as 'Braintree'.

As he was still in danger, a more influential Puritan, the 2nd Earl of Warwick, provided Hooker with a refuge in Holland, from whence he took ship. He sailed for America with his family on the *Griffin*, landing on 4 September 1633. At Boston he became pastor of the eighth church in Massachusetts. Two years later Hooker led a breakaway party of 100 men, women and children out of Massachusetts, 'driving their cattle before them for 100 miles through the wilderness, over mountains, through swamps, thickets and rivers, into the Connecticut River valley'. There they established a new colony and Hooker founded its first church. Having escaped from the plague in England he died at Hartford, Connecticut, a victim of an epidemic sickness in 1647.

Chelmsford remembers its curate with a memorial plaque: 'Thomas Hooker, 1586-1647, Curate at St Mary's church and Chelmsford Town Lecturer, 1626-29. Founder of the State of Connecticut, Father of American Democracy.' Quite an accolade.

With the American meaning of 'hooker', it is a point of historical pride and humour when citizens of Hartford insist they were 'founded by a Hooker...' (Considering the Puritan spirit, it is perhaps surprising that the Thomas Hooker Brewing Co. prides itself in supplying 'Connecticut's Beer'.)

Today there are Chelmsfords in Massachusetts, and in Ontario and New Brunswick, Canada.

AD **1537**

TREASURES
OF THE CHURCH

The Secret History of Moulsham

THE NAME MILDMAY was indelibly imprinted on the history of Chelmsford for almost 300 years.

Monasteries had been the cultural hubs for centuries, where learning and intellect thrived, arts and crafts were cultivated, good husbandry with animals, crops and fruit was developed and great architectural masterpieces of exemplary craft erected. In the process, some abbeys amassed considerable wealth, a fact that did not escape the grasp of a dominant monarch with his own personal agenda. At Henry VIII's behest, their coffers were plundered, their lands and buildings sold, and monks and nuns dismissed. Abbots who did not willingly surrender their domains were hanged, drawn and quartered.

Hospitals, like the leper hospitals at Moulsham and Maldon, lost their carers when monks and nuns were scattered, and while some men lost their heads, others – like Lord Rich (who gained Great Leighs and Rochford), Lord Petre of Ingatestone and Thomas Mildmay – made their fortunes and became the *nouveau riche* of the times. Lord Richard Rich turned a change of heart into a fine art, sending people to their deaths under Henry, burning them under Mary and hanging them under Elizabeth. Lord Petre oversaw the dissolution of religious houses, and the dismissal and sometime pensioning

off of the occupants. Thomas Mildmay, who died in 1551, was a successful merchant in the Chelmsford market. One of Mildmay's five sons, also a Thomas, obtained office as auditor to Henry VIII's Court of Augmentations, which was created in 1536 to manage and dispose of monastic lands confiscated by the Crown. He used his position well, acquiring land for himself, and in September 1537 he made his first acquisition, together with his father, acquiring the lands of the former Dominican Friary. Augmentation was especially apt for Thomas junior, for he soon augmented his private estate by acquiring a massive £622 5s 8½d. The estate was the manor of Moulsham, to the south of Chelmsford, which had been surrendered by Westminster Abbey that year (1539). Here he made his home, reconstructing Moulsham Hall in such a grandiose style that it was 'accounted the greatest esquire's building within the county of Essex'.

Towards the end of his life he enlarged his land holdings further by acquiring in 1549 the adjoining manor of Chelmsford from King Edward VI, which had been surrendered to the Crown by the Bishop of London in 1545, thus bringing the two manors together.

This Thomas Mildmay had eight children: four sons and four daughters. He died in 1567. Of his sons, Thomas,

THE HORRIBLE ROADS OF AD 1600
– KEMP'S 'NINE DAIES WONDER'

William Kempe (also Kemp) was an English dancer and actor specialising in comic roles, a contemporary and colleague of William Shakespeare. In February and March of 1600 he undertook his 'Nine Daies Wonder': long-distance Morris dancing from London to Norwich, the result of a bet. He was accompanied by a referee, a servant and a musician on the pipe and tabor. The journey took nine days, spread over nearly four weeks: 'Onward I went thus easily followed, till I come to Widford-bridge where a number of country people, and many Gentlemen and Gentlewomen, were gathered together to see me. Sir Thomas Mildmay, standing at his Parke pale, received gently a payre of garters of me…'

Gloves, points and garters were sold to finance his 'merry voyage'.

Chelmsfordians made so much ado at his progress it was with difficulty that he reached his inn: 'where I was faine to locke myselfe in my Chamber, and pacifie them with wordes out of a window insteed of deeds…'

He stayed on for rest and recuperation, until 'with hey and ho, through thicke and thin, the hobby horse quite forgotten, I follow'd as I did begin, although the way were rotten.'

Rotten indeed – so bad was the road out of Chelmsford, and so full of potholes, that one young lad among the people following him got stuck and had to be rescued by a friend and released from the water and mud: 'I could not chuse but lough to see howe like two frogges they laboured: a hartye farewell I gave them…'

Will Kempe performing his 'nine daies wonder'.

A memento of Chelmsford's once powerful and prolific Mildmay family ... the broken Mildmay Arms now on Chelmsford Museum's wall.

lived at Moulsham Hall (he had eight sons and seven daughters); William at Springfield Barnes; John at Cretingham in Suffolk; and Sir Walter at Apthorpe in Northamptonshire. From that time until the late eighteenth century Chelmsford was dominated by the fertile and successful Mildmay family, which spread and multiplied until late in the reign of James I no less than nine families of that name had amassed 'considerable estates' all over Essex.

Later, Moulsham Hall was rebuilt in the Georgian style by William Mildmay, who also (in 1758) rebuilt almshouses in Moulsham Street, that had been founded by Thomas Mildmay in 1545.

During the Napoleonic Wars, Moulsham Hall was leased to the army, after which it fell into disrepair. It was demolished in 1809. In 1839 the estate came up for sale, affording the wider expansion of Chelmsford. It's now a residential neighbourhood known as Moulsham Lodge.

VISITORS OF GREAT EXPENSE

Being a wealthy owner of property had occasional disadvantages. In Elizabeth I's time it meant the Sovereign might bestow on you the honour of coming to stay during her many 'progresses' throughout her realm. London in summertime could be an unpleasant place to be, with its smells in hot weather and outbreaks of plague in the tightly-packed city. Travelling abroad in the countryside would be a chance to escape all that, as well as making considerable savings on royal household expenses. That is, in spite of the royal baggage train of at least 300-400 carts. The whole entourage spanned, on average, a distance of 10 miles from the first wagon to the last, as her furniture, wall hangings, books, pictures, jewels, and bed-linen – including the royal bed – had to be moved with her for all the comforts of home. Elizabeth made in excess of 400 visits to individual and civic hosts between 1558 and 1603.

Entertaining the Queen was a great and prestigious occasion (if not always a welcome one, as it might cripple the owner's finances). In Essex, the Queen was entertained by Sir William Petre of Ingatestone Hall, by Sir Thomas Mildmay at Moulsham and Lord Darcy at St Osyth, among other great houses. At Horham Hall, Thaxted, she stayed for as long as nine days ... One Sir Thomas Mildmay is recorded as having ungraciously complained of the expense.

On 8 November 1638, England's doomed Charles I met his mother-in-law, Marie De Medici, the widow of Henry IV of France and mother of Louis XIII, at Sir Henry Mildmay's house, Moulsham Hall, when the unwelcome visitor had arrived at Harwich.

From Chelmsford, Charles escorted the formidable lady towards London. They rode in two long trains of coaches and horsemen: it is rumoured that Marie's household consisted of almost 600 Frenchmen, preceded by twelve trumpeters.

ATTACK OF THE WITCHES!

IMPS AND TOADS and dogs with horns, incest and communion with the Devil ... The charge was *Maleficium*, the use of diabolical power to cause harm – not heresy. The judgement was hanging.

With the Black Death a devastating and terrifying visitor, plus monumental religious upheavals, England in the sixteenth century was a frightening place. The Devil seemed to be getting the upper hand on earth, and to many it seemed only logical that there were some who sided with the evil one, and made pacts and wrought mischief (with his help); it was a time of poor medical knowledge and little help for the infirm and aged. Witchcraft was deemed the cause of every misfortune imaginable. Witchcraft, or the suspicion of it, thrived, and it was the poor old and vulnerable who became the scapegoats. Usually, this meant women.

King Henry VIII passed a Witchcraft Act in 1542, making witchcraft a felony (a crime punishable by death and the forfeiture of the convicted felon's goods to the state). Henry's second wife, Anne Boleyn, was accused of being a witch once he'd tired of her. The Act was repealed only some five years later under Edward VI, though by the time Elizabeth came to the throne witchcraft accusations once again permeated the land – and nowhere more so than in Protestant Essex. In 1562, Elizabeth passed a new Witchcraft Act.

This legislation outlawed all manner of 'Conjuracions, Inchauntmentes and Witchecraftes'.

About 229 people were indicted for witchcraft in Essex between 1560 and 1700, and some eighty-two Essex residents accused lost their lives at the end of a rope accused of this crime.

Life was perilous, with death a constant companion and the devil not far behind. Albrecht Dürer expressed the insecurity of the time (1513). (LC-USZ62-17351)

1566 – 1St Chelmsford Witch Trial, or 'The Examination and Confession of Certain Witches at Chelmsford in the County of Essex, Before the Queen Majesty's Judges, the 26th Day of July Anno 1566'

A witch and her familiars.

The first witches to be accused in a secular court in England resulted in a series of trials in Chelmsford, beginning in 1566. The first poor soul to be hanged for witchcraft was Agnes Waterhouse, but the first to be tried was Elizabeth Fraunces (Frances).

It was a strange story Elizabeth told in court. She first learnt the art of witchcraft, she told the astonished jurors, at the age of twelve, taught by her late grandmother, whose name was Eve of Hatfield Peverell. This trade caused her to renounce God and his word, and to 'give of her blood to Sathan', as she termed it. This Sathan was given to her in the shape of a white spotted cat. Her grandmother, Eve, taught her to feed the cat with bread and milk; she learned to keep Sathan in a basket. Elizabeth also confirmed that the cat 'spake to her... in a strange hollow voice', which she could understand.

She made many requests of 'Sathan'. Her first wish was to be rich, and in answer the cat brought sheep into her pasture 'to the number of twenty-eight black and white'. These sheep stayed for a time, but in the end 'did all wear away, she knew not how'. She then desired the well-off Andrew Byles for her husband. The cat promised to manage this, but stipulated that she first consent to Andrew's abuse of her, 'and so she did'. When he would not marry her afterwards, she fell into a terrible rage and instructed Sathan to 'first waste his goods' and then Andrew himself – whereupon he died.

In exchange for his favours, Sathan demanded a drop of her blood, for which she pricked herself in different places.

The red spots could still be seen when she appeared in court. When she suspected that she was with child, she willed the cat to destroy it. The cat then secured another less wealthy man for her, but again the proviso was for her to consent 'in fornication'. When a daughter resulted three months after their wedding, Elizabeth instructed the cat to destroy it, too, as it did not bring her the peaceful life she desired. The child died at six months. Next she required Sathan to lame her husband, and there followed a story of a 'toad-like' creature in his shoe which, when touched, rendered him lame, 'whereof he cannot be healed'.

After some fifteen or sixteen years, Elizabeth exchanged the cat for a cake from a poor neighbour, Mother Waterhouse, and passed on all the instructions she had received. Naturally, Agnes Waterhouse wanted to test Sathan's skills and bade him kill one of her hogs. The cat obliged, the price being a chicken and a drop of her blood. As time passed, Agnes' hands and face became covered in red spots where she had pricked herself so Sathan could suck her blood as payment for favours.

Agnes confessed to a string of misdemeanours involving the cat, such as having a neighbour and her own husband killed;

she always said 'her Pater noster in Latin' when asking for Sathan's services. She kept the cat in a pot on a layer of wool, but when she needed to use the wool (out of poverty) she turned the cat into a toad by saying the sign of the cross. Sathan had warned her 'she should have great trouble, and that she should be either hanged or burned shortly'.

In her own interrogation, Joan, Agnes Waterhouse's eighteen-year-old daughter, admitted her mother had tried to teach her 'this art', but she did not learn it. She saw Sathan once – when he was in the shape of a toad – and it was only then that she heard her mother call it by that name. She did confess that she once wanted to punish a neighbour's daughter who refused to give her a piece of bread and cheese and so called Sathan, who came to her from under the bed in 'the likeness of a great dog'. She told him she wanted to frighten the girl and offered a red cock as usual payment. He declined and instead demanded 'thou shalt give me thy body and soul'. Being 'afeared', she agreed and he frightened the other girl in the shape of an 'evil favoured dog with horns on his head'.

Agnes Waterhouse pleaded guilty and corroborated her daughter's story. When the attorney asked her 'How wilt thou do before God?' she answered: 'O my Lord, I trust God will have mercy upon me.'

'Agnes Waterhouse, when did thy Cat suck of thy blood?' asked the Queen's attorney. The jailor then 'lifted up her kercher on her head and there were diverse spots in her face and one on her nose...'

Before she was hanged at Chelmsford on 24 July 1566, Mother Waterhouse (sixty-three or sixty-four years of age) confessed she had been a witch for about twenty-five years, in which time she had practiced some abominable sorcery. Her daughter Joan was found not guilty. Elizabeth Frances was given a respite and was sentenced to the stocks and one year in prison.

1579 – THE SECOND CHELMSFORD WITCH TRIALS

The second outbreak of trials at Chelmsford involved 'A Detection of damnable driftes, practized by three VVitches arraigned at Chelmisforde in Essex, at the laste Assises...'

Again it was old Elizabeth Fraunces, along with several other women, who had to answer to the court. She had been short of yeast when she cursed one Poole's wife who refused to help her out. 'Presently there appered unto her a Spirite of a white colour in seemyng like to a little rugged Dogge', whom she told of her annoyance with the said woman and her wish to harm her in the head. She threw a crust to the little dog and Poole's wife suffered grievous pain in her head. (Most of the accusations at this sessions centred on the most banal crimes, with the most petty of motives.)

In turn, Elizabeth Fraunces accused several other women in the neighbourhood, sealing their doom as well as her own. Widow Elizabeth Lorde had offered a drink to a servant from Hatfield, who had died soon after. She had also bewitched another servant from Higham with a piece of apple cake – who, after eating it, died. And widow Mother Osborne was accused of having a mark on the end of a finger, and one on a leg, which had been 'pluckt out by her Spirit'; the late Mother Waterhouse (executed at the end of the case above), 'her owne sister', had the self-same marks. All three were found guilty and hanged.

Mother Staunton, late of Wimbish parish, was spared the rope as no crime could be attached to her, though she stood accused of many curious coincidences and connections in hindsight, when people or animals sickened after her passing.

Mother Nokes stood accused of causing a young man's lameness, so that he had to be sent home to bed in a wheelbarrow. The young man had – in jest – taken a pair of gloves from Mother Nokes' daughter and then ignored her entreaties to hand them back. 'Lette him,' she had said; 'I will bounce him well enough.' She was also accused of murdering a child by witchcraft.

1582 – ST OSYTH WITCHES TRIED AT CHELMSFORD

Here is another case, one – according to a source of the time – 'wherein all men may see what a pestilent people Witches are, and how unworthy to lyve in a Christian Commonwealth.'

Brian Darcy, chief interrogator of the St Osyth witches, was also the Lord of the Manor at St Osyth. As such, he would have been familiar with those brought before him, either accused or accusing. Sometimes they were both. They were the poorest of the poor. Once they stood before the court, finger pointing became an epidemic – many of the accused tended towards indiscriminate accusations, as if to find safety in numbers. Ursley (Ursula) Kempe even blamed one Ales Newman for having sent 'a spirit' to plague the late Lord Darcy to death!

Ursley Kempe, alias Grey, of St Osyth was sharp of tongue and friendless in her poverty. In February 1582, she found herself presented at Chelmsford before Brian Darcy, Esq., accused of being the cause of an infant's death. The child had fallen out of a cradle and broken her neck after her mother had refused to let Ursley be the nurse maid. Prior to that disagreement, Ursley had apparently improved the family's elder child's health; he had previously been unwell. The mother, Grace Thurlow, also confirmed Ursley had improved her own lameness after an agreed price of 12 pence – and that it had strangely returned when she was unable to pay for her treatment.

Annis Letherdall's evidence would seem too spurious for words. Ursley Kempe had sent her son to ask for a supply of scouring sand, for which she offered a task of work in return. Annis refused with an insult. Later, Ursley saw the daughter deliver sand to a neighbour, and had murmured something within earshot of the child. When the child fell ill, Annis accused Ursley of being the cause of it, which Ursley denied strenuously on her life.

Now it was Ursley's son Thomas Rabbet's turn to give evidence. He came up with four spirits or imps: 'Tyttey is like a little grey Cat, Tyffin is like a white Lambe, Pygine is black like a Toad, and Jacke is black like a Cat.' He confirmed he had seen his mother feed them with beer and a white loaf or cake and revealed that at night the said spirits would visit his mother and 'sucke blood of her upon her armes and other places of her body'. When his Godmother Newman paid a visit, his mother had given her an earthen pot in which he suspected

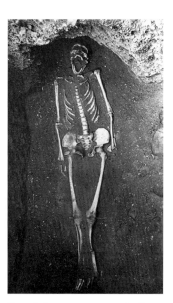

Two skeletons were unearthed in St Osyth in 1921. They had iron rivets driven through their elbows and knees – a practice intended to stop witches rising from the grave.

the spirits had been kept. A few days later he heard Newman say to his mother she had 'sent a spirite to plague "overseer" Johnson to his death, and another to plague his wife'.

Ales Hunt offered a tale of eavesdropping neighbours, suggesting Joan Pechey had entertained imps in her home when she knew there were no Christian creatures nearby. Widow Hunt informed the court that her mother had said, 'Joan was skilfull and cunning in witcherie', and knew what was said in any house in 'Saine Osees'. Once people's suspicions were roused, they were extremely inventive in finding accusations.

Ursley Kemp was called in her own defence. She admitted she knew of herbs and potions and had in the past successfully 'un-witched' those affected by the dark arts, but her tales of good deeds did not count for much: Brian Darcy then advised her to confess, saying 'she would have favour' if she did. On hearing this, she threw herself on her knees, weeping, and told him what he wanted to hear: by her confession it seemed that all illnesses, deaths and misfortunes in St Osyth could be laid at her door. She did not stop there, either, but listed the familiars and antics of other women in the village. Her interrogation lasted three days. 'Favour' was not forthcoming, and she was condemned.

Ales Newman admitted to calling Ursley Kempe a witch, but would not confess to anything incriminating, which obstinacy seems to have sealed her fate in the mind of Brian Darcy. She suffered the same fate as Ursley..

William Bonner told the court that his wife and one Elizabeth Bennet (*Pride and Prejudice* fans, take note!) 'were lovers and familiar friendes' and that Bennet had hugged his ailing wife and kissed her – and now his wife's upper lip was 'swelled and was very bigge...'. Together with Ursley Kempe's corroboration, that wild claim was enough to have Bennet arrested. However,

she refused to admit any knowledge of spirits, so a pot was brought into the court. This she admitted was hers – but not the wool it contained. She, too, was taken aside and promised 'favour' in exchange for a confession. Said Darcy:

> There is a man of great cunning and knowledge come over lately unto our Queenes Majestie which hath advertised her what a companie and number of Witches be within Englande: whereupon I and other of her Justices have received Commission for the apprehending of as many as are within these limites, and they which doe confesse the truth of their doeings, they shall have much favour: but the other they shall bee burnt and hanged.

Is there any wonder Elizabeth Bennet preferred to confess?

Annis Glascocke, a lawyer's wife, was accused of causing the death of children. When she was examined, spots were discovered on her thigh and shoulder similar to ones found on Ursley Kempe. Brought face to face, Ursley accused Glascocke. Annis retaliated by calling Ursley 'a whore' and 'a witch', who – she further claimed – had also bewitched her.

Ales Hunt was accused of keeping a spirit in a potsherd, as seen by Ursley Kempe. When the constable was sent to collect a milk dish from her house, supposedly used to feed her spirits, she denied it was hers, but when she was arrested she told the examiner in private that she had two spirits 'like unto little Coltes, the one blacke and the other white', called Jacke and Robbin. Then she accused her sister of keeping two spirits, 'like Toades, the one called Tom, and the other Robbin'.

Margerie Sammon, sister to Ales Hunt, denied a charge of 'entertaining spirits'; nor had her recently deceased mother been a witch, she insisted. Her sister then whispered to her in the court – and she broke down and claimed her mother (Mother Barnes) had given her two spirits on her deathbed, which she had taken home in a wicker basket. Subsequently she had taken them and released them, with instructions to make their way to Mother Pechey, saying: 'all evill goe with you, and the Lorde in heaven blesse mee from yee.'

Joan Pechey, when asked, suggested she was, 'threescore yeares and upwardes'. She denied any knowledge of spirits or such like. She also denied a suggestion of incest, of encouraging her twenty-three-year-old son Phillip Barrenger, 'to lye in bedde with her', saying he had sometimes lain on the bed 'at her backe'. Phillip himself admitted 'that manye times and of late hee hath layne in naked bed with his owne mother, being willed and commaunded so to doe of her'.

There were stories of carts that would not move past a supposed witch's house,

lockjaw caused by a disgruntled servant, a child dying because the father had accused someone of being a witch, cows that gave blood instead of milk, hogs that skipped, horses died at the plough and barns that caught fire.

A nine-year-old boy told of his mother's imps, 'with eyes like goose eyes'; they were called Herculus and Mercurie. His six-year-old brother confirmed his stories, but both parents denied everything. The mother, Cysley Selles, was condemned.

It is difficult to understand that the justices of the time would accept such trivia as truth or evidence, including the fantasies of children. All manner of witnesses claimed calamities had been caused by the women coming or going, often after years had passed between incidents. Here is one typical example: Margaret Grevell told the court that she had sent her son to John Carter of Thorpe,

Joan Prentis and her familiars, pictured beneath the three Joans on the gallows. (Museum of Witchcraft, Boscastle)

who had refused a request. After that, the brewing of his beer had to be aborted twice – in fact, until Carter's son shot several arrows into the brew, no doubt thereby killing the spell. Secondly, a butcher had refused her mutton: the milk for his workers' breakfast went off and stank, and cream would not turn into butter. Finally, a cow fell ill and had to be killed.

Disputes between neighbours would, in hindsight, be re-interpreted and the blame attributed to some past interaction with a vulncrable woman.

In spite of the promise of leniency, Ursley Kempe and Elizabeth Bennet were sentenced to hang. Four other women were found guilty but reprieved. Four more were acquitted, and two were acquitted but kept in prison. Only two were not indicted.

There were, however, voices of reason. In 1584, *The Discoverie of Witchcraft* was published by Reginald Scot following the Chelmsford witch trials. Reginald Scot argued that witches might not, in fact, exist.

1589 – YET MORE TRIALS AT CHELMSFORD

On the last day of March 1589 it was Anthony Mildmay Esq. who interrogated the latest batch of witches at Chelmsford, leading to: 'The Apprehension and confession of three notorious Witches, Arreigned and by Justice condemned and executed at Chelmes-forde, in the Countye of Essex, the 5 day of Julye, last past, 1589', and: 'The araignment and execution of Joan Cunny of Stysted in the Countye of Essex widowe, of the age of fourescore yeeres, or ther-abouts, who was brought before Anthony Mildemay Esq., the last day of March, 1589'.

Joan Cunny of Stisted seems to have confessed that she learnt the 'most detestable Arte of Witchecraft' from Mother Humfrye of Maplested, who taught her she must 'neele down upon her knees, and make a Circle on the ground, and pray unto Sathan the cheefe of the Devills'. When she tried that in a field, two imps appeared with her in the circle, looking like two black frogs. They would do her bidding and she promised them her soul in return. She had four principal spirits, all specialists: Jack killed men; Jyll killed women; Nicholas killed horses; Ned killed cattle. Joan had somewhat of a reputation: 'This Joan Cunny, living very lewdly, having two lewd Daughters, no better than naughty packs, had two Bastard Children, beeing both boyes'. Both these illegitimate children were called as witnesses, the eldest being about ten or twelve years of age.

Joan Upney was brought before Sir Henry Gray on 3 May 1589. She had killed with the aid of moles and toads.

The Devil visited another Joan, Joan Prentice, at night in the shape of a ferret with fiery eyes, demanding 'Joan Prentice, give me thy soule'. Satan's name, this time, was Bidd. She refused to give her soul, but let the fiery being drink some of her blood from a finger and from her cheek. For that, the ferret would do harm to whomever she desired.

All three Joans were found guilty by the jury on 5 July 1589, charged with causing the deaths of men, women and children and committing 'very wicked and horrible actions divers and sundrye times'. No time was spared – no more than two hours later they were transferred to the gallows, where they died 'with penitent hearts'.

Of Joan Cunny's 'lewd' daughters, Margaret received a year in prison and six terms in the stocks, and daughter Avice was found guilty, but claimed pregnancy. She was hanged a year later, after the birth of her child.

FORBIDDEN PLEASURES OF THE SIXTEENTH CENTURY

THE CONCEPT OF sport, at least where the lower classes were concerned, used to be a problem in Tudor times, when most games and sports were forbidden. (Though with low earnings and meagre incomes, obesity would hardly have been a problem then ...)

Football was expressly forbidden by a succession of Kings, but that does not seem to have stopped teams from one village or town from challenging another, even if the goal posts might be miles apart. If peasants had surplus energies they were supposed to use them in service of their masters. Gentlemen and yeomen, however, could not so easily be restrained.

Unfortunately, misadventures will happen and fatalities occurred, even with the best of intentions, at trials of strength and speed. The statement 'without malice' turns up again and again in cases of sporting accidents.

FATALITY AT CHELMSFORD WRESTLING

During a bout of 'playing and wrestling' in Coneyburrow Field, Chelmsford, in 1572, 'for the sport of it and without any malice', William Egham, gentleman, and Thomas Hewys, yeoman, aged thirty, both of this town, faced each other in a trial of strength. Death claimed his victim when Hewys put his arms about Egham's waist to lift and unbalance him. In the struggle and tussle they both fell 'with great force' and Hewys's head received such damage that he died the following day. The jury

Albrecht Dürer also expressed the other side of the coin: to live for the day, for tomorrow we may die ... (LC-USZ62-127107)

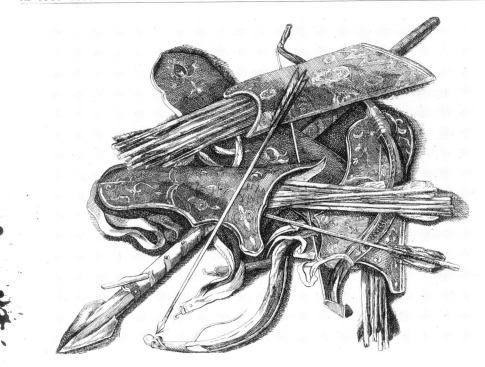

Bows and quivers of the sixteenth century. (With kind permission of Thomas Fisher Rare Book Library, University of Toronto)

recorded a verdict of accidental death, but Egham had to wait ten months for his pardon.

FENCING WITH STICKS

Even a young peasant's version of fencing with 'single-stick', known as wasters, could have its deadly consequences. Richard Ingolle of Epping, aged fourteen, encouraged Henry Campe, a yeoman and friend, to take up one of his bundle of sticks and join him in play. Campe accepted one 'without any evil intention'. During their game, Campe struck Ingolls under the right ear, a blow that meant instant death for Ingolle. A plea of not guilty was recorded in an inquest in 1592.

DANGERS OF ARCHERY

Edward II felt that football interfered with the defence of the realm in 1314, which would be better served by archery. So he passed a law banning football and ordering all men earning less than 100 pence a year to purchase a longbow. Every village had to provide an area for men to practice on. It was said that when a young man could hit a squirrel at 100 paces he was ready to join the King's army. (Football was still ok for the upper classes, though.)

Archery being compulsory, the victory at the battle of Agincourt proved English archers were most effective when facing an enemy. Training, however, took place locally 'in the butts', usually on the village green or common. We still find names like Buttsbury and Butts Green harking back to those days. Before the rules of 'Health and Safety' mollycoddled the populace, the butts could be dangerous places.

In Stisted, one evening in June 1566, a labourer shot an arrow from one butt to another. A two-year-old girl got in the way of the arrow, which entered her eye. She died a week later. Again, the inquest stated that the incident happened without any malice and the archer was pardoned that year. At a practice by the young men of Little Oakley parish in 1579, one young archer shot another, aged just sixteen, also in the eye. The victim died the next day. Another archery death occurred in 1581 during practice at Barking town butts, when a bystander was fatally wounded.

HUGH BARKER – 'BARBER, SCRIVENER, TOOTH-DRAWING AND BLOODLETTING'

Cuckolding seems to have been a favoured pastime in old Chelmsford. Geoffrey Chaucer wrote his sometime saucy *Canterbury Tales* at the end of the fourteenth century; Chelmsford's saucy tales began over 100 years later, in October 1601. Alas, it wasn't their literary merit that preserved them to this day, but the fact that some of the characters ended up in court, captured for posterity in the Chelmsford hundred's jury report.

Barber-surgeon Hugh Barker duped a poor schoolmaster from Boreham into turning a story he told him into a saucy ballad. Soon it 'was being recited in every beerhouse in Chelmsford'.

Mary, wife of tailor John Whale, the brother-in-law of John Pope, a glover, were slanderously mentioned in it: 'And if her husband takes him at the fray /
Up goes his hose and fast he runs away…'

Another line had this to say: 'Called Mary White that bonny lass / But her husband is a very ass…'

Various characters from Chelmsford society were mentioned, and the outrage grew. It got so bad that the barber tried to bribe and bully his way out, but to no avail: it came to court. The judgement read, 'Guilty, to be imprisoned for one year and in the interim, and to be placed in the pillory in four markets, viz.: Chelmsford, Witham, Braintree and Billericay and to pay to the Queen £40.'

The barber of Chelmsford was obviously a slow learner, for even after that he was indicted again. In 1618 he was outlawed.

Clement Pope left his buff doublet to John Whale in his will of 1598, perhaps a token of remorse for the liberties he had taken with the celebrated Mrs Whale?

Barker the barber was by no means the only one at the mercy of the crowds in the stocks in Chelmsford. In 1576 Robert Taswood, a brewer of Chelmsford, was put in the stocks (though his offence was not recorded).

Chaucer's Canterbury Tales *were echoed in Chelmsford 100 years later. (LC-DIG-highsm-03162)*

SWIMMING ON BLADDERS

In 1576 a group of boys were, with many others, swimming in the millpond at St Osyth. One boy attempted to swim with the aid of two inflated pigs' bladders – we would call them waterwings today – tied to his body for buoyancy. As he began sinking, he called out: 'I am drowning! I am drowning! For the love of God help me!'

That may seem an awfully long sentence for someone at the point of drowning… Two boys gallantly came to his rescue, but their feet slipped and all three of them were lost. It is interesting to note that the coroner's inquest found it necessary to set the worth of the bladders at 1 penny. Swimming with inflated bladders was not unusual. Shakespeare mentions it in Henry VIII: 'Little wanton boys that swim on bladders'.

Other pastimes, not strictly games, could also be dangerous:

PLAYS were not classed with games in the sense of the statute and were allowed, dependent on the strength of the local Puritan influence. Towns and villages would put on their own religious plays and native drama flourished, especially in a town like Chelmsford, where 'handsome profits' could be collected. Plays even contributed to the repair of a bridge at Sandon. People would have struggled to get some joy into their lives and there are reports of Whitsun church ales, May Days, children's Christmas plays, even Morris dancing, Corpus Christi and the plough feasts that had survived from Pagan times.

FAIRS were held once or twice a year in most market towns and also some villages, and many fell on Saint's Days or Sundays, which meant large-scale absenteeism from church. The detractors went to work: 'little else [is] bought or sold in them than good drink, pies and some peddlery trash'. Fairs ought to be abolished, they said, particularly as they led to 'the corruption of youth, who must needs repair unto them whereby they often spend not only the weekday but the Sabbath in great vanity and riot'. If it was fun it had to be bad – and suppression of disorderly fairs was sought by the more sober-minded parishes in petitions to the Quarter Sessions (or directly to the justices). In 1578, juries for several Hundreds in Essex prevented fairs held on Sundays on three separate occasions. For landowners, that meant a loss of income. In 1580, 'a fair kept on Sunday in Chelmsford' on the first of May was petitioned against. We do not know if Puritans won the day.

ROUGH JUSTICE

JUSTICE WAS HARSH in the past, especially on poor people, with judges donning the black cap and sentencing prisoners to death by hanging for comparatively mundane reasons. Records of many of the cases of the Essex Assize Courts sitting at Chelmsford allow glimpses of justice at its most brutal. Among the following judgements, only one of the accused was set free.

> Breaking and entering; sheep, boar and horse stealing; thieving; a highway robbery, which took a grand total of 3 shillings and 'a hat worth twelve pence' – plus of course a few feet of rope, which was free.

There is also infanticide, a women killed in a brawl with another woman – and bestiality. All sentenced to hang. One unlucky chap was even sentenced just for harbouring 'the intention to steal'. Here are a few of the capital cases:

- ✼ 26 July 1566: Thomas Wayer of Bradwell-next-to-Sea broke into the house of William Fleminge of Wratting and stole twenty-one pieces of cloth.
- ✼ 3 March 1575: John Yonge of Purleigh broke into the close of John Lock at Hazeleigh and stole a grey gelding (a castrated horse).
- ✼ 12 January 1576: Thomas Andrewe of Latchingdon stole a sorrel (reddish brown) gelding at Purleigh belonging to Thomas Kynge and a black gelding at Mundon.
- ✼ 13 March 1587: Ralph Johnson of Stow Maries stole £5 7s 6d in money, three silver rings, a silver pin, a 'fustian doublet' and other items from William Munte at Althorne. It seems a poor haul to die for.
- ✼ 2 March 1592: Thomas Rampton of Purleigh stole twenty-one sheep from James Osborne at North Fambridge and

Is he the hog-herd or a hog thief? Justice was rough and the hangman's noose often stretched for very small offences. (LC-USZ62-84264)

Chelmsford's old County Goal was demolished 1559. (Reproduced by courtesy of the Essex Record Office–I/Mb 74/1/169)

three heifers from Edward Webbe at Colchester. Rampton had previously been allowed 'clergy'. (Benefit of clergy was an exemption of clerics from trial in a civil court. In time this meant anyone who could read, usually from the Bible. In some cases the prisoners learnt the chapter by heart. That avoidance of the death penalty could only be allowed once, though.)

- 12 March 1592: George Osborne of Hazeleigh stole a boar belonging to John Argent. He, too, was a re-offender. A year earlier he had been allowed 'clergy' for six thefts of livestock, so the court ran out of options.
- February 1597: Francis Parker of Cold Norton broke into the house of Henry Mildmaye between 6 p.m. and 7 p.m. and stole a 'freese coate' (probably a warm one?), a doublet of fustian, two breeches and a shirt, all belonging to William Brayford.
- 5 November 1597: Jesper Harman of Earls Colne was accused of breaking into the house of John Saunders at Woodham Walter between the hours of 4 p.m. and 5 p.m. and stealing a pair of breeches, a 'frieze jerkin', two pairs of stockings, a hat, a waistcoat, a shirt, three ruff-bands, seven falling-bands, a sheet, three 'pillow beers', five kerchiefs, two silver rings, a silk girdle, two smocks and four cheeses. Rather surprisingly, perhaps, Jesper Harman had luck on his side, and he was reprieved.
- 27 February 1598: Robert Berdsell of Woodham Mortimer stole a sorrell dunne gelding 'worth 60*s*', belonging to Ralph Cortman. He died for a horse ...
- 27 February 1598: Richard Warde of Inworth broke into the house of Nicholas Johnson, clerk, at Woodham Mortimer, between 1 a.m. and 5 a.m., while Nicholas Johnson and his household were 'being therein'. Warde stole a black cloak, four 'neckerchefes', three 'crosse clothes', three 'coifes', two 'holland bandes', one table cloth, three 'napkyns', a pewter ewer, six pieces of pewter, two 'candlestickes of latyn'

and a 'posnett of brasse', a 'chafyngdyshe of latyn', a 'morter with a pastle', a 'greate rybb of beafe', a 'legg of porke', a 'foreloyne of porke' and a 'brest of porke'. (With all that brass and pewter and the joints of meat to carry out, the Johnson household must have consisted of deep sleepers.)

✖ 1 January 1610: Thomas Last of Southminster broke into the house of Agnes Evans, widow, in the daytime and stole some money, a silver ring and a pair of stockings. The total worth was just 9 shillings, or less than a pound.

✖ 14 March 1610: Richard Fisher of Woodham Mortimer broke into the house of William Harrys, knight, and stole 'fower paire of sheetes' and 'a velvitt cull'.

✖ 24 July 1615: John Pidgeon, alias Damon of Althorne, stole two pairs of stockings, 'a silver whissell' and some money from Robert Tiffen.

✖ 26 June 1638: Joan Caston of Mundon was delivered of a bastard male child whom she strangled.

✖ 28 February 1676: Elizabeth Glascock of Purleigh struck and kicked Elizabeth Williams upon the chest and stomach, giving her 'a mortal bruise of which she died'.

✖ Those of a delicate disposition might want to avoid this one... 31 August 1685: John Raynor of Purleigh committed 'buggery with a bitch'.

At the Midsummer Assize in 1609, held at Chelmsford and lasting three days, fourteen prisoners were executed at Rainsford End. At the Lent Assize the following year there were twenty-two. All of them were interred in Chelmsford churchyard.

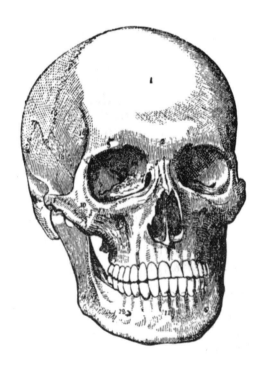

AD **1648**

FOUL CRIMES DURING THE CIVIL WAR

PARLIAMENT CREATED THE Eastern Association as 'an organization for the mutual defence of Cambridgeshire, Essex, Hertfordshire, Norfolk and Suffolk' on 20 December 1642. Oliver Cromwell joined as colonel of a horse regiment the following year and was promoted to lieutenant-general of horse the year after that.

By then that army, commanded by the Earl of Manchester, was one of Parliament's largest field armies. In the spring of 1645 it was merged into the New Model Army.

When, in May 1648, the county of Kent rose in revolt against Parliament,

A Royalist cavalry charge recreated – the Sealed Knot in action. Chelmsford was taken and abandoned again on the route to Colchester.

Lord-General Fairfax's Roundhead forces recaptured Maidstone. Remnants of Royalist forces, led by George Goring, 1st Earl of Norwich, regrouped in Essex. Chelmsford stood for the King, and a Royalist uprising that has been described (by Parliamentarians?) as 'a riotous croud' took the Essex County Parliamentary committee prisoner on the 4 June.

Sir Charles Lucas seized Chelmsford and took command of the Essex regiment. On 9 June he marched with a total force of around 4,000 troops to Braintree, where the county magazine's weapons had already been 'liberated' by the northern Essex Trained Bands, who had remained loyal to Parliament. Lucas continued to Colchester, arriving on 12 June. Fairfax followed. The Siege of Colchester lasted from 13 June to 27 August.

In that turbulent year, as proved in the Calendar of Essex Assizes for 1648, a few facts stand out: most of the offences before the judges concerned either food (or potential food) or horses and almost all of the accused were 'labourers' (with the addition of a few 'spinsters'). With armies on the prowl, provisions would have been at a premium. In the general confusion, several of the accused had absconded by the time of their trials.

✗ On 19 March 1649, two families appeared in court at Chelmsford charged

53

SISSIES ON PARADE

A curious 'tradition' was brought back from the annals of history on Sunday, 22 May 2011, when dubious characters, cross-dressing in the fashions of the English Civil War, paraded the modern streets.

According to the legend, the event started 'when the Royalist Commander of Chelmsford and his men were made to parade through the town in women's dress by the Roundheads they'd just surrendered to'. We cannot vouch for this tradition, as certainly on one occasion the townsfolk abused the Roundheads (who surrendered to them). It is true, though, that Chelmsford avoided much trouble, unlike our neighbour Colchester. The event is immortalised on a Turner Prize winning exhibit by Chelmsford artist Grayson Perry. The 'Chelmsford Sissies' vase can be found in the town's museum.

with fighting to the death over 'rootes and turnips in the ground'. Robert Baisey and his son William tried to steal the turnips; Daniel Nightingale and his son John were the turnips' defenders. John punched William, at which the elder turnip thief got hold of John 'by his doublett, collar and his haire and laid hold on his staffe with a knife in Baisey's hand and threatened to cut his throte'. Terrified, the young man struck out – and killed Robert Baisey with his wild blow. The verdict, luckily, was self-defence.

✳ 1 January 1648: John Sellinnes and Henry White, both Hawkwell labourers, stole 'three white hogs'. Luckily for them, they could not be brought into court; unluckily for them, this was because they were 'both [already] dead'.

✳ 20 February 1648: Richard Challice jun. of Sturmer, labourer, about 3 a.m. broke into the house of Robert Taylor and stole 30lbs of port, twelve loaves of bread, and a pair of gloves. He pleaded not guilty. Richard senior managed to find an 'Ignoramus' (Solicitor), and his son was acquitted.

✳ 24 February 1648: Math. Pickett of Navestock, labourer, stole 5lbs of port,

6lbs of sugar, 5lbs of currants and three cheeses. He was whipped.

✳ 12 October 1648: Nathaniel East of the parish of St Mary, Colchester, labourer, stole 100lbs of woollen yard, fifteen cheeses and a sack. He was branded.

✳ 12 November 1648: John Moonson, labourer of Little Thurrock, was indicted of stealing a bay gelding, a 'fleabitten' gelding, a dun gelding, and a grey mare; on 2 January 1649, meanwhile, labourer Robert Scurle of Great Walden (Saffron Walden) stole three ewes and five wethers (castrated male sheep). The simple entry says 'Escaped'.

✳ One of the luckiest fellows at the time was George Haley, labourer, of Walthamstow. He was indicted on three separate occasions: on 28 February 1648 for stealing three bushels of oats; on 6 March 1649 for stealing two white ewes; and on 14 March 1649 for stealing an iron chain. On each occasion he pleaded not guilty and was acquitted.

✳ 20 January 1649: Jonathon Fayers, glazier, was found guilty of and hanged for the murder of Edmund Allum at Thundersley with 'a soldering iron'.

AD 1645

THE WITCHES RETURN,

or Death by Imp!

WHEN JAMES **VI**, King of Scots, also became King James I of England, he brought his zeal for witch hunting with him. In 1604, Elizabeth's Act was broadened, encouraging a new wave of persecutions. This was the statute under which Matthew Hopkins, the self-styled Witch-Finder General, operated and which he turned into a profitable business in the midst of the confusion of the Civil War.

In the inquisition at Chelmsford on 25 March 1645 we find among those giving evidence two names that would strike fear and loathing into people in the east of England at the time and are still reviled to this day. They are Matthew Hopkins, Gent, of Manningtree, and Master Sterne (Stearne); both were employed by the court as investigators.

Hopkins had the knack of making the most innocent of occurrences sound sinister and turned everyday situations into damning evidence. He had found his calling. Once you were in his sights, it was difficult to escape.

Up before the court that day was Elizabeth Clarke, alias Bedingfield. Her mother and others of her family had already suffered 'death for Witchcraft and Murther', yet when those two 'investigators' visited her in her home she seems to have actually hastened her own doom. She told the wicked pair that a plump white dog with sandy spots and short legs in her presence turned into 'one of her white Impes', called Jarmara, and a greyhound called Vinegar Tom became an imp 'in the shape of a Greyhound with long legges'. Soon the poor Elizabeth Clarke compounded the evidence by admitting to the two informers:

> ... she had had carnall copulation with the Devil six or seven yeares; and that he would appeare to her three or foure times in a weeke at her bed side, and goe to bed to her, and lye with her halfe a night together in the shape of a proper Gentleman, with a laced band, having the whole proportion of a man, and would say to her, Besse I must lye with you, and shee did never deny him.

Elizabeth then revealed another witch in Chelmsford, mentioning five imps of her own and two imps belonging to Anne Weste, widow. Sometimes Elizabeth's imps would suck 'of the old Beldam' (a hag or a witch) and sometimes Anne's imps sucked on Elizabeth. The imps would be sent out to kill hogs or horses of neighbours in the village.

Matthew Hopkins had his own evidence to offer, of two strange cases that occurred on the same night he interviewed Elizabeth: his own greyhound had chased a kitten, but the kitten had fought

Pets might get you killed at the Chelmsford Witch Trials. One accuser with little imagination suggested that only the devil could invent names like these.

back and injured his dog; then a black cat – 'onely it was thrice as big' – had stared at him and then run off when his greyhound chased it, opening a gate to escape. Hopkins made this sound most suspicious. John Sterne added a few more imps to Hopkins' account, all seemingly dogs: Hoult, Jirmara and one called Sack and Sugar. When asked if she was afraid of her imps, the old lady answered: 'What, doe yee thinke I am afraid of my children?'

Many people gave evidence, much of it hearsay, assumption or speculation. Four women recounted three recent local deaths, all blamed on Anne West by Elizabeth Clarke. They had watched with her, and at 12 a.m. she had smacked her lips and 'a white thing about the bignesse of a Cat' appeared, along with five imps. Several others also corroborated these stories.

One witness had visited the old woman in prison and enquired about his brother's death at sea. A hoy had sunk and his bargeman brother drowned thirty months earlier; Elizabeth Clarke, he said, had blamed Anne West for raising that wind.

Two other women were accused: Anne Leech and Elizabeth Gooding (who allegedly cursed a horse to death after its owner sold her a pound of cheese). Cows died in the street near the home of Anne Leech, and a child had died in the neighbourhood of Clark and Gooding. The Chelmsford women must be to blame, as 'this Informant doth verily believe'.

Anne Leech in turn implicated others in her examination. They had sent an imp each to have someone killed – or someone's wife or daughter, or indeed some horses. She stated that her health had only been good when she sent out her imps to do mischief, imps who 'did usually suck those teats which were found about the privie parts of her body'. A curious observation is the natural acceptance by the women that these 'imps' spoke to them and they could understand them, like children might accept fairy stories.

The words 'imp' and 'pet' seem to have been interchangeable. Helen Clark, the daughter of Anne Leech, called her familiar Elimanzer, but she strenuously denied having caused anyone's death.

Prudence Hart blamed Rebecca West and Anne West, her mother, for her miscarriage. Rebecca West, daughter of Anne West of Lawford, had confided some tales of a young man or young men who had been familiar with her and lain with her 'in the likenesse of a proper young man, who desired of her' and he/they had promised to avenge her on her enemies. Now a young man had died …

Rebecca West, Anne West, Anne Leech, Elizabeth Gooding and Helen Clark of Mistley had all met at the house of Elizabeth Clark, where they each exhorted their imps with their desires and wishes, which largely consisted of some hurt or misfortune to another.

Matthew Hopkins visited Rebecca West at Colchester Castle, where she was kept with the other five, until the next gaol delivery. Young Rebecca had confessed to Hopkins they had all met at Elizabeth Clark's house, where she had been made to promise 'that shee must never confesse any thing, although the Rope were about her necke, and shee ready to be hanged'. She promised and the Devil came into her lap and kissed her and within six months he turned up just as she was about to go to bed and he 'told her, he would marry her, and that shee could not deny him; shee said he kissed her, but was as cold as clay, and married her that night...' They had walked about the room plighting their troth.

A more sinister and bizarre development, of which Hopkins made good use, was the engagement of females to search the bodies of accused witches for the tell-tale signs of communion with imps. As no two human bodies are the same, discrepancies could be found and misinterpreted. Birthmarks, liver spots, moles and warts became suspect. Elizabeth Hunt and Priscilla Brigs found that Mary Greenleife 'had bigges or teates in her secret parts'. Mary Greenleife had been suggested as a suspect by a former friend. When asked how she came by those teats which were discovered in her secret parts, Mary Greenleife answered she 'knew nothing about them, unless she were born with them'. She also denied ever to have entertained any imps to suck on these teats. She did, however, confess she had seen a leveret once sitting before her door, within a yard of the threshold. Suspicious indeed!

One of the female witch inspectors was a midwife. She 'found such Marks, or Bigges in their privy parts, that she never saw in other women: for Sarah Hating had foure Teats, or Bigges in those parts, almost an inch long, and as bigge as this Informant's little finger ...'

At least four deaths were blamed on Sarah Hating, largely because a snake had been found and chased at her house.

Another of the women said, of Margaret Moone of Thorpe, that 'she found three long teats or bigges in her secret parts, which seemed to have been lately sucked...' When she searched the accused's daughters, she found 'two of them had biggs in their privy parts as the said Margaret their mother had'. When challenged, the said Margaret was unable to make her imps materialise and she denied everything that was said about her.

In some cases, the accused, under severe stress, began to mutter what can only be described as gibberish. Margaret Moone recited, among the names of her twelve imps, Jesus, Jockey, Sandy, Mistress Elizabeth, and Collyn ... Sarah Barton's imps, meanwhile, were called Littleman, Pretty-man, and Dainty. Even a minister of Clacton, Joseph Long, stood up in court and added to the witch mania by retelling a 'confession' of one Anne Cooper, who had 'three black Impes suckled on the lower parts of her body'; these went by the names of Wynowe, Jeso, and Panu. (She had also sent an imp to kill a child in Clacton.)

Imps might be a toad or a bird, even a lamb or a young hare or a squirrel, as small as mice or as large as a greyhound. Sucking on the nether regions had become folklore, and this was claimed by many of the accused, as was sending them off to harm someone or someone's animals – the remuneration in blood was often a common denominator. Killing a child might be revenge for having been refused a pint of milk. Imps tended, as we have seen, to have names, from the most common (like Tom) or the most obvious (like Frog), to quirky inspirations. If their testimony is to be believed, handing out, sharing or passing imps or pets on, even from mother to daughter, was widespread.

MATTHEW HOPKINS (C.1620 – 12 AUGUST 1647) – WITCHFINDER GENERAL?

Exodus 22, verse 18: 'Thou wilt not suffer a witch to live …'

Matthew Hopkins, with his sidekick John Stearne, is believed to have been responsible for the deaths of around 300 women between the years 1644 and 1646. It is difficult to be accurate, but in the confusion that was during the English Civil War he claimed to be officially commissioned by Parliament to uncover and prosecute witches, although that never happened. It gave him power over intimidated people. Towns would welcome him to rid them of imagined witches and gladly pay him to do so. He outlined his witch-hunting methods in his book, *The Discovery of Witches*, which was published in 1647.

Torture was illegal in England, but Hopkins got around that as his methods were mainly bloodless: sleep deprivation, employing women to 'prick' the skin and facilitate intimate searches of the accused's bodies, searching for blemishes, birthmarks, warts, anything that might be construed as giving succour to the Devil.

The profitable, if gruesome, activities only lasted about a year and a half: not much time to have amassed such notoriety. In fact, Hopkins' life was much shorter than those of most of his victims. He died at his home in Manningtree on 12 August 1647, only about twenty-seven years old, probably of pleural tuberculosis. He was buried a few hours later in the graveyard of the church of

MATTHEW HOPKINS.

Some curious or preposterous reasons were found by Matthew Hopkins and his helpers to condemn the innocent to death. Here a supposed witch is swum...

St Mary at Mistley Heath. So the story of his being put to his own method and killed is probably just that, wishful thinking.

Of thirty (or thirty-two?) witches tried, fourteen (or nineteen?) were hanged at Chelmsford on Friday, 25 July 1645, '... there being at this time a hundred more in severall prisons in Suffolke and Essex'. The names of those that were executed were: Mrs Wayt, a minister's wife; Anne West; Mother Benefield; Mother Goodwin; Jane Browne; Mother Forman; Rachel Flower; Mary Greene; Mary Foster; Jane Brigs; Mother Miller; Mother Clarke; Frances Jones; Mary Rhodes.

King James I's Act remained in force until 1736.

RETURN OF
THE BLACK DEATH!

THERE STILL WAS no cure for the plague when it returned in the sixteenth century. It came mysteriously, took its victims and disappeared again, only to return another day. This unpredictability made death a constant companion. Severe epidemics of the plague broke out again in Essex in 1504 and 1518, and again between 1543 and 1546.

Burials were not always reserved for churchyards. In 1665 the dead were so numerous that orchards and gardens might sometimes be the nearest and quickest venues for disposal. Many corpses were interred hurriedly at night.

Sir Ralph Verney's letters reveal his refusal to even house his own relatives in order to forestall possible infection in the seventeenth century. When the plague reached Chelmsford and threatened the Verneys, self-preservation took priority over neighbourly aid. Sir Ralph's correspondence reveals that men from the surrounding area stood 'with guns redy to shoot them if they stur,' and women 'hardly dare visit one another if sick'.

An entry in the churchwarden's book at St Mary's Church (now the cathedral) indicates that Christian charity and mercy were in short supply: 'Paid for powder and shott delivered [to] ye watchmen to keep Mousam (Moulsham) from coming to bury theire infected dead in ye churchyard, 1s 8d.'

Did vigilantes keep out Moulsham's plague victims? The people of Moulsham, without a church or chapel of their own, would have tried to bring their dead to sacred ground ...

The Black Death had returned intermittently over the centuries, but in this era it must have seemed as if Armageddon itself had arrived. Here the Four Horsemen of the Apocalypse – Death, Famine, War and Plague – trample all before them.
(Dürer, c.1497-98) (LC-USZ62-84269)

A LAZARET FOR PLAGUE VICTIMS

In seventeenth-century Venice, the plague killed one third of the population, wiping out 50,000 people out of a total of 150,000 in just one year. A 'lazaret', a quarantine colony to help prevent the spread of infectious diseases, was established on the island of Lazzaretto Vecchi, which has been found to contain several centuries of mass graves from the late fifteenth century onwards.

Archaeologists discovered in 2006-7 that about 500 people a day used to die there at the height of an outbreak. Conditions were far from modern standards. 'It looked like hell...The sick lay three or four in a bed,' wrote the sixteenth-century Venetian chronicler Rocco Benedetti. 'Workers collected the dead and threw them in the graves all day without a break. Often the dying ones and the ones too sick to move or talk were taken for dead and thrown on the piled corpses.'

Female 'vampires' were blamed for spreading the disease. Bricks have been found placed into the mouths of skeletal victims to stop them rising and practicing their perceived aberrations.

Chelmsford had its own dead. The household of the Cock Inn, which stood next to the bridge (now a large store instead) lost several of its members. Tradition tells that victims from the Cock Inn were buried in the grounds.

The Sewells murdered a guest for his money at the Shears, Chelmsford. Here Death calls to collect his share of the loot. (With kind permission of Thomas Fisher Rare Book Library, University of Toronto)

The former landlady of the White Horse in the High Street, Mrs Sewell, was running the Shears, now the Two Brewers in Springfield Road, when she fell ill. It must have seemed like divine retribution, for together with her husband she had murdered a guest, Thomas Kidderminster, while she was landlady at the Shears. The motive had been greed. Mr Kidderminster had been murdered for the £600 he carried with him on his travels. He was buried in the orchard – though when Wesleyan Chapel Sunday Schools were built on what used to be the grounds of the inn, no proof of this legend was found.

Further outbreaks of plague visited in 1603, 1625, 1637 and 1666. Travellers might carry the disease with them (and Chelmsford, of course, straddled the London to Colchester Road). Still, the town did not fare as badly as Colchester, where one in eight of the citizens was struck down in 1665. Daniel Defoe mentions in *A Tour Through England and Wales* that Colchester lost 5,259 people to the plague that year, 'more in proportion than any of its neighbours, or than the city of London'.

By 1700, Chelmsford had a population of about 3,000.

BURNING, HANGING AND PRESSING IN THE EIGHTEENTH CENTURY

HIGH TREASON WOULD result in hanging, drawing and quartering for men, but burning for women, for quartering women would have involved female nudity. High treason included counterfeiting money or coining and clipping (removing the rims of coins of silver or gold to produce new coins, as well as colouring coins to pass for higher values). But there was also petty treason, the murder by a woman of her husband or her mistress, as they were considered her superiors in law. For women convicted of either high treason or petty treason the sentence was burning at the stake in public. Of course they would be drawn publicly on a hurdle to their place of execution, quite often passing the gallows on their way, where condemned males might already be hanging – and preferably on a busy Market Day for maximum deterrent effect.

One such unfortunate creature was Margaret Onion, who was brought before the court at Chelmsford for poisoning her husband Samuel. Under 'Country News', the *Chelmsford Chronicle* in 1735 recorded her ordeal in a short statement: 'On Thursday last Margaret Onion was burnt at a Stake erected near our Gallows, for poisoning her Husband; she was a poor ignorant illiterate Creature, and confess'd the Fact.' What her 'superior' husband had done to provoke such treatment at her hands was not stated. Four men were

hanged as well that day at Chelmsford, but they did not even merit a mention in the news. Was Margaret Onion strangled before the faggots were lit beneath her, or did she suffer the slow death of burns and flame and smoke inhalation? Prior strangulation was, by that time, an accepted mercy. Not even the date is certain; one source states that she died on Friday 8 August that year.

Margaret Onion was burnt alive in Chelmsford. It became an accepted part of death by burning, that a rope would mercifully strangle a victim to death before the faggots were lit. It did not always work.

Highwaymen became the stuff of legend, but were they really this well dressed? If caught, not pleading might get you pressed.

Mary Brewer, on 29 March 1746, and Phillis Dykes, on 4 August 1749, were both hanged here for the murders of their male bastards. Phyllis Dykes died in the company of two male convicts.

Frances Cheek was hanged on 12 August 1754 for the murder of her daughter, Hester.

Elizabeth Holmstead, on 22 November 1782, and Clare Montford, on 26 March 1790, paid with their lives for burglary.

That same year, on 5 June 1790, hanging was substituted for burning as penalty for petty treason by Act of Parliament.

HIGHWAY ROBBERY

The *Ipswich Journal* of Saturday, 2 April 1763 carried the following news item:

Chelmsford, March 31. Last Friday Samuel Sorrell was executed here pursuant to his Sentence for robbing Mr Stonard on the Highway, as mentioned in our last. He heartily asked Forgiveness of his Prosecutor, who, at his earnest Request, attended on the morning of the Execution. He acknowledged the Justice of his Sentence; earnestly caution'd the Spectators to shun the ensnaring Crimes of Drunkenness and Fornication, that led him to the Commission of that for which he suffer'd; and died, to all Appearance, truly penitent.

Then the paper added another Chelmsford snippet, one that seems to indicate that even highway criminals could have a heart: 'We hear that a Sailor was robbed last Tuesday on Widford Bridge, near this Town, by two Footpads, who took from him 10 Guinneas, and gave him back two Shillings to bear his Expenses.'

THE TERRIBLE 'PEINE FORTE ET DURE'

The pressure on your chest is becoming unbearable. Your staccato breath quickens under the load and, although the weights are only on your chest, it feels as if they're pressing down on your face, such is the pressure on your veins, which rise up, blue and swollen. They want to burst. You want to move, but your hands are tied and your feet spread-eagled to the four corners of the dungeon-like room. You faint, but not for long enough, before your breath bursts forth again.

It's the law's way of trying to force you to plead – but if you do, you will be found guilty, your family will have to live with the shame of your criminality and you will forfeit your worldly goods. You want to leave them to your children, so you try to take it, but your body can't ... Then they're putting on more weights. And more.

Your lips are dry. You will not drink until tomorrow, and then only the worst water they can find. That drink alternates with the stale lump of bread you are offered once every other day. Eventually, if you don't change your mind, your ribcage collapses...

In 1767 a Chelmsford highwayman would not confess:

He [that] is judged mute, that is dumme by contumacie... his condemnation is to be pressed to death, which is one of the cruellest deathes that may be: he is layd upon a table, and an other uppon him, and so much weight of stones or lead laide uppon that table, while as his bodie be crushed, and his life by that violence taken from him. This death some strong and stout-hearted man doth choose, for being not condemned of felonie, his bloud is not corrupted, his lands nor goods confiscate to the Prince ...
(Sir Thomas Smith, *De Republica Anglorum*, 1583)

Eventually he pleaded not guilty, but he was convicted and executed – and then hung in chains for good measure. From 1772, 'standing mute', the refusal to plead, was treated as equivalent to a guilty verdict, eliminating the need for pressing. Finally, an Act of 1827 ruled that 'standing mute' be henceforth taken as a plea of not guilty.

SECRETS OF THE BODYSNATCHERS!

Crimes and Misdemeanours in Georgian Chelmsford

THE ASSIZE SYSTEM has its origins back in the twelfth century. By the middle of the sixteenth century six such circuits had evolved, each under the control of the Clerk of the Assize. They were normally held twice a year in Lent and summer, occasionally with an additional sitting in December. In counties where the Assize was an annual event, the accused might have to languish many months in prison awaiting trial.

In the eighteenth century judges rode on horseback from county town to county town, trying in turn all the people who had been charged with more serious criminal offences, those the magistrates or the Quarter Sessions could not deal with. Quarter Sessions coped with the lesser, non-capital crimes and were held four times a year in each county. The system of Assize Court and Quarter Sessions lasted until 1971, when it was replaced by the present Crown Court system.

HORSE THIEVES BEWARE

Today thieves target cars and motorbikes. Prior to the advent of motor transport the horse was a necessary and valuable commodity. In March 1754 the landlord of the White Hart at Brentwood offered half a guinea reward to anyone with information about 'a little man, pretty talkative with a large mouth and small face', who had hired 'a roan mare to go to Chelmsford' and ridden off with it. Newspapers regularly carried advertisements offering rewards for the apprehension of horse thieves.

Village or parish constables, often illiterate and unable to outsmart the devious and determined villains, were pretty inadequate in upholding the law, not to mention the wide-reaching task of forestalling and recovering. Wealthier people found other ways to protect their properties. On 17 August 1770, the Saracen's Head in Chelmsford was the venue of one such meeting, when gentlemen, farmers and others banded together to form an association 'for the apprehending and convicting of horse stealers within the said hundred'.

Other similar associations colluded about the neighbourhood. Watchmen were hired, and substantial sums were paid out as rewards for information as well as covering the prosecution costs. Subscriptions at £40 might be the carrot to sow disloyalty among thieves. Some horse owners took to patrolling their districts themselves. Horse thieving was reduced somewhat, but not stopped. Horses stolen in Kent might come up for sale in Essex (and vice versa). There have always been those who preferred an easy shilling to an earned one.

In 1839 an Act of Parliament encouraged counties to establish police forces to 'combat crime and lawlessness'.

Waiting for Napoleon

'**FRANCE MUST DESTROY** the English monarchy, or expect itself to be destroyed by these intriguing and enterprising islanders ... Let us concentrate all our efforts and annihilate England. That done, Europe is at our feet ...'

These words of Napoleon echoed through the shires in the aftermath of the French Revolution of 1789. England and France were at war almost continuously from 1793 to 1815, and there were real fears that the 350-mile Essex coastline was being earmarked for invasion.

National contingency plans were drawn up and it was decided that King George III would come to Chelmsford if the French landed in Essex, along with the Prime Minister and the Home Secretary. The Queen and the King's daughters would cross the River Severn, and take refuge in the Bishops' Palace at Worcester.

A militia was raised by ballot. Parish constables had to present lists of men eligible to serve, usually those aged between eighteen and forty-five. Lists were posted on church doors. Reluctant men could appeal if they had a valid reason. In Chelmsford, such reasons included 'being deaf', 'having five children under age' and being 'blind in one eye and weak in the other'.

In 1797, landowners with more than ten horses were required to provide one mounted soldier to form a local cavalry unit, but to begin with Essex's fighting force was woefully ill-equipped: there were wildfowling guns, axes, billhooks, pitchforks ...

Meetings were held in the Shire Hall on 3 April 1798 for the purpose of forming the volunteers, and it was decided that its purpose was to 'be faithful and bear allegiance to his majesty King George III (and him will defend) to the utmost of our power against all conspiracy and attempts against his person, crown and dignity by the hostile attacks of foreign enemies or the wicked designs of seditious and disaffected persons.' They also vowed 'to serve during the present war and for 6 months afterwards.' Their resolve: 'Be ready whenever our service is required'.

A judges' procession up High Street in 1762, in all its pomp and tradition. The sixteenth-century session house at the top, witness to so many witch trials, was replaced by the Shire Hall in 1791. The lauded Black Boy Inn (centre right) is a clothes shop now. (Image courtesy of Chelmsford Museum)

On 9 April 1798, Thomas Frost Gepp was elected captain, John Oxley Parker Jr was elected first lieutenant and George Welch was second lieutenant. A captain was appointed to exercise the soldiers. Drill days were to be Mondays, Wednesdays and Saturdays.

Unfortunately, Robert Strutt, having provided himself with a uniform and being elected a member of the corps, refused to sign the roll of conformity (agreeing that he would abide by the rules), 'having neglected to attend drills several weeks previous' to his being reported sick. It was unanimously resolved that Mr Strutt's conduct was highly inappropriate, disrespectful to the corps, and his name was 'expunged' from the books.

For others it was an honour to be part of the corps. John Seaman was taken on as a drummer at 6 pence per week. Charles Hollingsworth enlisted as 'piper', but was unable to provide himself with a uniform; he was clothed out of 'the corps' fund'.

Preparations on the ground were also progressing. In order to block an advance on London from a possible landing on the Essex coast, barracks were built in several places in and around the town. The *Ipswich Journal* of Saturday, 10 September 1796 reported: 'upwards of 200 men are working almost night and day at our new barracks'. A barracks occupied the site of the old friary at the town end of Moulsham Street, accommodating 4,000 troops of the 44th East Essex Regiment.

Defensive fortifications were planned and construction supervised by the Royal Engineers to the south of Chelmsford in 1803. This included two star-shaped

Right: 'Emperor' Napoleon in all his glory. His imperial throne is supported by the Imperial Eagle (bottom left), one of which was snatched by the 44th East Essex Regiment of Foot at the Battle of Salamanca in 1812. It is now displayed at the Essex Regiment Museum. (LC-USZC2-2871)

Below: Return from Invasion – contemporary cartoon showing 'Boney' returning to France, tattered and woebegone. An English soldier kicks the Napoleonic posterior. (LC-DIG-ppmsco-07204)

THE DREADED LASH!

Flogging was a common punishment in the Army during the latter part of the eighteenth century. As many as 500 or 1,000 lashes could be applied for the most trivial offences as recently as 1812, when a General Order limited the number of strokes that could be ordered by a regimental court-martial to 300.

After 1832, more than 500 or 600 lashes were rare. In 1808, one incident alone saw several men who had attempted to desert sentenced to a gruesome 1,000 lashes each. As five seconds was slowly counted between each lash, the punishment lasted three hours and thirty minutes.

The martial laws of England were described by many as 'the most barbarous in Europe'. A flogging could be so severe that men were often disabled for life. Sometimes they died under the punishment.

A contemporary description gives some idea of the brutality of the old flogging with the cat-o'-nine-tails:

Henley, for desertion, received 200 lashes only. Acute inflammation followed, and the back sloughed. When the wounds were cleaned, and the sloughed integuments removed, the backbone and part of the shoulder-bone were laid bare. Another man was taken down, at the recommendation of the medical officer, after he had received 229 lashes, and sent to the hospital, where he died in eight days, his back having mortified.

The offender is sometimes sentenced to 1,000 lashes. A surgeon stands by to feel his pulse during the execution, and determines how long the flogging can be continued without killing him. When human nature can stand no more, he is remanded to the prison (hospital), for from the shoulders to the loins it leaves him one wound [which] is dressed, and, as soon as it is sufficiently healed to be opened in the same manner, he is brought out to undergo the remainder of his sentence.

---

artillery forts on the ridge south of Moulsham, one at Widford (commanding the Clacton Road) and one at Galleywood, on the racecourse astride the Margaretting road, blocking the Maldon Road and hopefully protecting London's north-eastern flank.

From a small county town with a fair share of trade and judicial traffic, Chelmsford suddenly found itself host to more men than it could regularly keep abreast of. Local papers were keen to report on all military movements. The *Ipswich Journal* of 27 March 1795 reported that 'our barracks are beginning to fill, upwards of 500 officers and privates are lodged in them and 700 more are expected in them everyday.'

On Saturday, 3 November 1798, it was reported that the 4th Division of Surrey militia 'marched into our barracks; and yesterday the 1st division of the Northumberland militia marched into the old barracks: our garrison is now augmented (with) 105,000 effective men.'

Right: '48 hours after landing!' –
British caricaturists made short shrift of
Napoleon. Here is an 1803 vision of what
John Bull would do to him, should he dare
to cross the water. (LC-USZ62-112)

Below: Bonaparte and the
French armies imagined fleeing
the defending regiments!
(LC-USZ62-111311)

The Sevastopol Cannon, a reminder of another conflict, the Crimean War of 1853-56. Now at Essex Regiment Museum, it used to stand near the Shire Hall until 1937.

Troops marched through or were billeted at Chelmsford on their way to Colchester and then on to Harwich, so that soldiers sometimes outstripped the accommodation Chelmsford Barracks could provide. A newspaper report of 13 April 1798 described the situation:

The regular barracks at each wing of this town being full of troops, new ones are ordered to be run-up with all possible dispatch for the reception of 3,000 more infantry. The commander in chief of the eastern division has sent quartermasters to requisition all the principal barns, granaries, etc in and near the town for the immediate recommendation of a large body of troops which are ordered for that coast.

In Chelmsford as a military thoroughfare, crime rose, along with gambling and drunkenness – from both soldiers and civilians alike. Military punishments for such crimes were often severe. Here is a story from *Ipswich Journal*, 11 August 1797:

Yesterday two private soldiers of the 49th Regiment of Foot in our new barracks were committed to the county gaol for violently assaulting and committing rape on the body of a young woman of this town who was walking with a lad in the parish of Springfield on Tuesday evening last. The soldiers kept the lad prisoner alternately upwards of 2 hours while they committed the horrid act. The two men were recruits who had lately joined the regiment from Chatham; they had since their arrival robbed their comrades and deserted, for which each received 400 lashes and were then turned over to the civil power.

In 1810 a householder complained of unbecoming behaviour of militia men in the guardroom opposite to where they lived.

In the years after 1795 – and up to the victory at Waterloo – there was an unending stream of companies entertained at the popular Black Boy Inn, but in the year 1800 *The Gentleman's Magazine* carried the following horrific report:

A fire attended with most calamitous circumstances broke out on Monday evening at one of the stables in the Black Boy Inn, Chelmsford. Several hundred Hanovarian soldiers halted that night in the town and its vicinity and from the great numbers billeted on the Innkeepers they were compelled to lodge them in the stables and out-houses; those quartered at the Black Boy had retired to the stables allotted them with their pipes and it is supposed that the fire dropping from one of them communicated to some loose straw which set the premises in a blaze.

By the activity exerted by all ranks on the occasion the conflagration was prevented from extending beyond the premises but we are sorry to add 24 of

Napoleon and Josephine feast upon England – from plates containing the Bank of England, St James', and the Tower – whilst the hand of God declares judgement on the French forces: you have been weighed, you have been measured, and you have been found wanting. (LC-USZC4-8790)

Britannia between Death and the Doctors. Here an ailing Britannia is approached by Death in the guise of Napoleon, while her politicians squabble. (LC-USZC4-8794)

the soldiers are missing, 15 of whose dead bodies were dug out on Thursday.

Chelmsford's old and 'infamous' watering hole, the Black Boy Inn, formerly the Crown Inn, at the junction of High Street and Springfield Road, was a staging post on the Colchester-Harwich road. It had been renamed the Black Boy in the sixteenth century and served as post office since 1673. Early in the eighteenth century it was pulled down and rebuilt. It was always popular, however, and frequented by the great and the good. Charles Dickens mentioned it in his *Pickwick Papers*, and the Duke of Wellington changed horses here. It is thought to have had a brewery.

Napoleon never attempted his planned invasion, and the preparations and the Loyal Chelmsford Volunteers were never put to the test. Although the war was not to end until 1815, the corps was consigned to history in 1809.

The defence works were decommissioned around 1813. Much was destroyed by the construction of the London-Chelmsford railway line in the middle of the nineteenth century, but battery earthworks survive on Chelmsford Golf course and Galleywood Common. Only street names remind of the barracks today, and the many pubs that sprang up during this period to cater for thirsty infantrymen.

Convicted to be transported ... to Van Diemens Land?

Essex responded immediately. The new paid police force was not alone in reducing this crime. The advance of the railways and then motorcars considerably reduced the value and need for horses.

FREE JOURNEYS TO AUSTRALIA AND VAN DIEMEN'S LAND

There was another solution to the punishment of unwanted criminals: transportation. The new colonies needed workers – and what better way to save on the upkeep of villains in jails than simply banishing them from the realm? Unauthorised returnees would meet with the death penalty.

Labourer Simon Moulds reached the Chelmsford Lent Assizes on 8 March 1797 at the age of twenty. Together with one William Presnall (or Presnell), he had unleashed a miniature crime wave, and the pair stood accused of four separate offences of cattle stealing. Both were found guilty, and sent to 'be hanged by the neck until [they] be dead'. They seem to have claimed a different home address for every felony. Both were young men and the colonies needed people, so their sentences were commuted to transportation for life.

Together with a number of others, the two offenders exchanged the gaol at Chelmsford for the *Barwell*, a ship waiting in the river Thames, bound for New South Wales. 'Death and Casualties by Sea excepted', they would spend the rest of their lives in Australia.

In about 1802-1804, Moulds took up a relationship with another convict, a young lady who had arrived from Gloucestershire in 1790, at the age of about sixteen. She already had three children from three previous relationships, yet the remarkable story is that she had been blind for some years. The couple were to have four children of their own and were to remain together for the rest of their lives. Simon Moulds became a landholder and left a fifty-acre farm to 'Ann Davis, now Mrs Moulds' in his will of 1839.

Simon's co-accused, William Presnell, ended up in Tasmania, where he had some success with farming and other commercial interests.

John Hutt was born in about 1811 in Chelmsford (he claimed). Over a period of three and half years, from 1827-1830, he had been caught and found guilty of at least five offences before he was transported to Van Diemen's Land (Tasmania), where he added at least another twelve offences to his name. He had started with minor misdemeanours like stealing shoes and ducks and worked up to stealing cattle, which attracted a death sentence. This was reprieved to transportation for life in 1830.

He spent three months on the Portsmouth hulks. Described as having a 'bad character', he sailed on 26 May 1831 on a voyage of 105 days, arriving on 1 November 1831. He was not easily subdued, spending weeks in irons and in chain gangs, but eventually he settled down, married Martha Hodgson in 1845 and fathered nine children. John Hutt died on 26 October 1872; his body rests in Van Diemen's Land.

Bodysnatchers at work by candlelight.

DANGER! RESURRECTIONISTS AT WORK

Early in the nineteenth century, the search for answers and the increase of knowledge of the medical/surgical profession exposed an anomaly in the law that made it possible to disinter and abscond with a dead body, facing only a small fine or short sentence if caught.

Chelmsford Assizes dealt with a case of body snatching on 15 January 1822. William Crouch was found guilty of a misdemeanour 'in opening a grave and carrying away a dead body.' He received just three months in prison.

James French of Waltham Cross received twelve months in prison for a similar offence in January 1827.

The case of Sam Clarke shows the disparity in the law. His horse and cart were traced by the landlord of St Anne's Castle public house, John Crisp, and the toll collector, John Redwood, following the grisly discovery of a young woman's naked body in a field by Little Leigh's parish church. Hugh Simmons, the church-warden, also noticed a nearby horse and cart, a shovel and a sack with a brace of pistols. A box on the cart still carried the odour of human remains. A grave had been disturbed in the churchyard, and close by was found a small crowbar.

Samuel Clarke admitted three charges of removing bodies, but those charges do not seem to have been followed up. Instead he was found guilty of theft and sentenced to be transported for seven years. The naked body in the field was that of Joanne Chinnery, who had been buried five days earlier in her best clothes, including her favourite gown. It was their theft that convicted Sam Clarke.

The medical profession relied on such nefarious means for their research and training, while relatives and friends of deceased mounted nightly vigils at grave-yards until such time as decomposition made a corpse valueless to the resurrec-tionists. Graves had to be secured with heavy stone slabs or bound with iron bands to forestall thefts of their contents.

The *Chelmsford Gazette* reported a trial of body snatchers in 1825, where even the judge was affected by the pain of relatives of the exhumed, which caused him to comment that 'if experience and skill could be obtained only by such means, it might be better if ancient ignorance might return'.

A NEW JAIL AT SPRINGFIELD

In 1826-27, Chelmsford got its new jail. The last public execution at Moulsham Gaol took place 28 July 1826, when Isaac Smith was condemned for bestiality with an ass. The first execution at the new Springfield Gaol – or as the *Chronicle* described it, 'the new drop' – followed on 10 December 1828, when Reuben Martin, alias James Winter, paid the ultimate price for the murder of Thomas Patrick in a drunken brawl:

> On getting into the van, the shouts of the populace were tremendous and deafening; he bowed, and with a smile threw his hat into the air, exclaiming, 'You may go, I shan't want you again.' The chaplain tried to get him to confess. His execution for murder was unjust, he declared, though he agreed he deserved to die, 'for he had committed hundreds of robberies'. He would not snitch on others, so he would not confess. The body, after hanging the usual time, was cut down, and delivered to the surgeons for dissection.

The youngest person ever hanged at Springfield Prison must be James Cook, a cow-hand aged sixteen, who was executed on 27 March 1829 for arson, having set fire to the premises of farmer William Green, his employer.

DEATH FOR MURDER AND ATTEMPTED MURDER ONLY

The year Queen Victoria came to the throne, 1837, was also the year most reasons for execution (capital offences) were quashed, reserving the death penalty only for murder and attempted murder. The latter was abolished in 1861, leaving only murder, treason, espionage and arson in the Royal Docks on the statute books as grounds for capital punishment in public.

Twenty-seven murderers fell foul of the hangman's noose in Chelmsford during Queen Victoria's reign, plus one would-be murderer. Among the victims of those crimes were eight girlfriends, seven wives and one husband.

While executions for murder were carried out until 1964 in England and Wales, the last hanging in Chelmsford took place in 1914, when one of the oldest persons ever to face execution, seventy-one-year-old Charles Frembd was hanged for murdering his wife Louisa.

THE CHELMSFORD TREADWHEELS

⸺᪥⸺

The Devil makes work for idle hands. Idle prisoners are an unproductive resource. In the nineteenth century much ingenuity and enterprise went into devising machines to combine that notion with punishment when hard labour had to be provided. The treadmill was installed in Chelmsford's house of correction in 1822 by the inventor William Cubitt from Ipswich. It was a simple if terrifying machine, based on the wheel. Normally wheels would supply power to grind corn or pump water, but in this case the power was not supplied by a gushing brook but by human effort. Parties of prisoners would be constantly stepping and ascending the never-ending wheel, easily supervised and always monotonous. Chelmsford's machine had two wheels, housed in separate yards – one for male prisoners and one for female – though such labour was later withdrawn from female convicts.

⸺᪥⸺

ABOLITIONISTS AND SLAVES

IN 1783, WHEN the Society for the Abolition of the Slave Trade was formed, its organisation was exclusively male. Even abolitionists like William Wilberforce were opposed to women's involvement. To some ladies that just was not good enough. A Chelmsford woman, Anne Knight, was one of the first activists. She advocated the abolition of slavery, and set up a branch of the Women's Anti-Slavery Society in Chelmsford in 1830.

This society was disbanded after the Abolition of Slavery Act was passed by Parliament in 1833 and Anne Knight turned her attention to other worthy causes, like factory reform, ending the Corn Laws and Parliamentary reform. Together with other activists she was involved in the Moral Force Chartism movement. Her involvements and struggles demanded frequent visits to London, where she worked with abolitionists like Thomas Clarkson. In 1834 she toured France, giving lectures on the immorality of slavery. She argued for immediate abolition without compensation.

When, in 1840, attempts were made to stop women delegates from taking part in the World Anti-Slavery Convention in London, Anne Knight was so outraged that she began a campaign advocating equal rights for women. Seven years later she published the first ever leaflet on women's suffrage. One of her ploys was to attach colourful printed slogan stickers to the outside of her letters.

Her contribution to the anti-slavery campaign was later recognised when a village for Jamaican freed slaves was named Knightsville.

Anne Knight (1786-1862) was born the daughter of a Chelmsford wholesale grocer, a Quaker family of pacifists, deeply involved in Anti-Slavery and Temperance campaigns. She was described as 'a singular looking woman – very pleasant and polite', yet she was tenacious. In 1851

Anne Knight spent her life campaigning, against slavery, and for women's rights. (Courtesy of Library of the Religious Society of Friends in Britain)

Above: *The Great Anti-Slavery Meeting, which refused to let Anne Knight in!* (LC-USZ62-133477)

Right: *The dreaded lash tears open a slave's back. At the mercy of his or her owners, a slave's life was of commercial value only.* (LC-USZ62-41839)

she helped establish what is believed to have been the first British association for women's suffrage, which held its first meeting in Sheffield.

In 1846 she moved to France, participating in the revolution of 1848 and attending the international peace conference in Paris in 1849. Her eloquent letters admonished churchmen and politicians in the cause of women's rights, reminding them of the biblical words: 'Do unto others as thou wouldst have others do unto thee.' She died in France in 1862. In Chelmsford, Anne Knight House, one of the 'new Houses' at the University of Essex, carries her name.

NEW ORLEANS TO FREEDOM

Joseph Freeman was an 'Iron Foundryman' in the Iron Works in Chelmsford's New London Road. On 12 October 1863 he married Sarah Farrow, a forty-two-year-old widow, at the Old Meeting House, Baddow Lane. He was about thirty-five years of age. There is nothing unusual in that – except that Joseph had been born in New Orleans, Louisiana, in America's Deep South in about 1826, a slave and the son of a slave. He had escaped his shackles in around 1861. On arriving in England, he settled in Chelmsford. Was it Anne Knight's legacy that attracted him? Or maybe it was Chelmsford's industry? Joseph and

AN EYE-WITNESS ACCOUNT

In 1846, Samuel Gridley Howe, an American pioneer in the education of blind and handicapped children, had occasion to visit a prison in New Orleans. He wrote about what he saw in 'a large paved courtyard, around which ran galleries filled with slaves of all ages, sexes, and colours'.
Most of them, it seems, took little or no notice of the public flogging in progress.

I heard the snap of a whip, every stroke of which sounded like the sharp crack of a pistol... There lay a black girl flat upon her face, on a board, her two thumbs tied, and fastened to one end, her feet tied and drawn tightly to the other end, while a strap passed over the small of her back, and, fastened around the board, compressed her closely to it. Below the strap she was entirely naked. By her side, and six feet off, stood a huge negro, with a long whip, which he applied with dreadful power and wonderful precision. Every stroke brought away a strip of skin, which clung to the lash, or fell quivering on the pavement, while the blood followed after it.

Her master had brought her in for punishment – no questions asked, just so long as the lashes 'were short of twenty-five'. Alternatively, the owner could have done the brutalizing himself by installing a private whipping-board on his own premises.

'Erected by his Christian friends to the memory of Joseph. Once a slave in New Orleans, who escaped to England and became also a Free Man in Christ...' (28 November 1875). Joseph Freeman's gravestone.

Sarah had seven children, though there were also twins who both died as babies. The two eldest daughters were silk winders (probably in the silk works in Mildmay Road that was to become the Marconi factory).

Joseph Freeman died of consumption (tuberculosis), aged only about forty-nine, on 28 November 1875. In 1881 his widow, Sarah, lived at No.55 Moulsham Street with another daughter called Sarah (fifteen), both working as sack makers. Sarah senior died in 1906, aged seventy-nine, in Moulsham Street almshouses. Both Sarah and Joseph lie buried in the New London Road Cemetery. His monumental inscription adds: 'once a slave in New Orleans / who escaped to England and / became also a Free Man / in Christ / He was employed... / at the London Road Iron Works.'

As a slave, Joseph would have carried the name of his owner, which is not known. 'Freeman' would seem an appropriate description for a man to adopt who managed to escape slavery at the start of the American Civil War. The US exploited some 1.775 million slaves in 1860, out of a total population of about 14.5 million. In Louisiana, about 47 per cent of the population were slaves at the time. The average sale price for prime male slaves in 1861 was $1,381.

AD 1776-1846

EVEN QUEEN VICTORIA COMPLAINED ...

GOOD JUDGES, NOBLE judges, and downright evil ones have sat in judgement at Chelmsford, from Sir Robert Tresilian and his 'Bloody Assizes' to the reformer Sir Nicolas Conyngham Tindal (1776–1846).

Born in Chelmsford, on a site marked today with a commemorative plaque at No.199 Moulsham Street, Judge Tindal's name stands out among lists of legal experts for the considered verdicts he gave, judgments that have influenced the legal system to this day.

Nicolas Conyngham's family lived at Coval Hall, Chelmsford, for three generations. Robert Tindal, his father, was a Chelmsford attorney and the Revd Nicolas Tindal, his great-grandfather, was the translator of the *History of England* by Paul de Rapin. With all probability, another famous personality among Tindal's forebears was William Tyndale, the translator of the Bible.

From King Edward VI Grammar School in Chelmsford, Nicolas Conyngham's education transferred to Trinity College, Cambridge, where he graduated eighth wrangler (a mark of excellence) in 1799 and was elected fellow in 1801.

After years of practicing in the interesting job description of 'special pleader', in 1810 he was called to the Bar in Lincoln's Inn, like many of his ancestors before him. He certainly displayed his

learning, as he did in the curious case of Ashford v Thornton, a murder trial from 1818. As counsel in the appeal he argued – successfully – that Thornton was entitled to the ancient opportunity of 'trial by battle'; his opponent's client refused to take up the challenge, and thus he won his case. The law was changed afterwards, and this is the last time this defence has appeared in an English courtroom.

Tindal served as solicitor general, followed by another office he held with distinction, that of Chief Justice of the Court of Common Pleas. He introduced

Sir Nicolas Conyngham Tindal. Born in Chelmsford. (Courtesy of Chelmsford Museum)

In Tindal Square the statue of Sir Nicolas Conyngham Tindal sits brooding opposite the Shire Hall (c.1911).

the special verdict of 'Not Guilty by reason of Insanity' or 'Guilty but Insane', and the defence of provocation.

One of these sensational verdicts was brought about by the case of Daniel M'Naughten in 1843, a Scottish wood-cutter who murdered the secretary to the Prime Minister, Edward Drummond, mistaking him for his master. Under Judge Tindal, the jury found him 'not guilty by reason of insanity' and he was acquitted. Queen Victoria herself called for the case to be retried in the House of Lords, but the Lords' review – based on Tindal's advice – upheld the court's verdict, and the precedent is still in use today.

Of Tindal and his wife Merilina's four children, Louis Symonds Tindal became Vice Admiral and the Revd Nicolas Tindal became rector of Chelmsford. Sir Nicolas Conyngham was buried in Chelmsford and is commemorated by a plaque inside the cathedral.

THE QUEEN CAROLINE AFFAIR OF 1820

Of such enormity were the debts of George, Prince of Wales, that he was persuaded by Parliament to marry his cousin, Caroline Amelia Elizabeth of Brunswick-Wolfenbüttel (1768-1821). It was a disaster waiting to happen. One of his other mistresses was sent to meet the new bride when she arrived at Greenwich prior to the nuptials. The prince is said to have been drunk on their wedding night and it went downhill from there, though there was a daughter, Charlotte Augusta. Shortly after her birth, the royal consort moved out of her apartments in Carlton House.

The prince then set in motion a system of spying on his spouse in order to find reasons for a divorce and instigated such persecution of her person that she moved abroad for a period of time. On returning to this country for her husband's coronation, while the people welcomed her, the prince had the doors of St Paul's Cathedral shut on her and his friends set about bringing her down. The government colluded. The machinery of Parliament would be invoked to try her without having to involve the courts, where the prince's own affairs and conduct might be open to investigation.

Counsel appearing for and against the bill represented a formidable array of legal talent, including three future chancellors and two future chief justices. Nicolas Tindal was a junior defence counsel. In the end the bill was withdrawn and the queen's party claimed an unmitigated victory. The eleven weeks of the trial and her successful defence gave a considerable boost to Tindal's career.

WICKED MURDERERS HANGED AT CHELMSFORD!

THE HANGING OF DRORY AND CHESHAM

It promised to be quite a spectacle when William Calcraft was called upon to perform a double execution at Chelmsford prison, using his 'short drop' method.

Some 6,000 or 7,000 spectators had been gathering from 6 a.m. in the morning in the space between the gaol and the chief police station opposite, 'consisting principally of smock-frocked labourers, their highlows and gaiters spattered with mud, and their steps heavy with the number of miles they had travelled to the hanging', reported the *Observer* (on 31 March 1851).

Horrible and Bar-bar-ous Murder of Poor
JAEL DENNY,
THE ILL-FATED VICTIM OF THOMAS DRORY.

Thomas Drory committing his vile crime upon poor pregnant Jael Denny.

People had come from all parts of the surrounding countryside. A few farmers were present, 'eyeing askance the dismal implement above the jail gateway.' Above the murmur of the crowd 'the calls of orange vendors might be heard at intervals'. The paper took the high ground: 'There were hardly any respectable people observable in the crowd, but a most disgusting number of women. Some of these had gay flowers in their bonnets... others were mothers, giving suck to infants whom they carried in their arms; others were elderly matrons...'

The condemned they had come to watch paying the ultimate price for their crimes were quite unconnected, quite different personalities, yet they were a man and a woman, a seducer-murderer and a husband-poisoner ...

Drory, a farmer's son, had seduced a servant girl, Jael Denny. She had expected to be married, but when she was 'far advanced in pregnancy' he lured her to a dark and secluded spot and strangled her. The evidence was irrefutable, in spite of his 'ordinarily mild deportment, effeminate looks and small person', yet even in the face of the clearest evidence, he insisted on his innocence – until, that is, at the last moment, the Monday night before the Tuesday morning execution. At his and his father's request the text was not to be published, though it is known that he tried to make some amends by asking that his money – £8 11s 4d – was handed to the girl's mother as some kind of 'part restitution for the grievous injury' he had caused her. He also hoped that, as an example, his just death would deter others from committing so wicked and horrid a crime. The letter, dated Springfield Jail, 24 March 1851, revealed a large degree of illiteracy.

Drory also admitted, in his last moments, that the child Jael Denny had been carrying was his. He had met the girl by chance on the evening of the murder, and arranged a later meeting. Then he went to a cellar in his father's house and collected a part of a rope he knew had been left there. When the lovers met again that fateful evening, she urged him again to marry her. He managed

Printed in Chelmsford in 1851, obviously a rush job to be sold to the crowd.
'Life trial confession and execution of T. Drory and S. Chesham, Trials Broadside 232,' Courtesy of Harvard Law School Library
http://nrs.harvard.edu/urn-3:HLS.Libr:912791)

to slip the rope around her unnoticed until the end was in the loop. Then her hands flew to her throat as she jumped up in terror, but it was too late! He pulled hard and she sunk, mute, to the ground ...

Drory left her lying there and went to Brentwood. One witness stated afterwards: 'I saw the cord around her neck; it was turned around three times, and she had one end in her hand. Her face was swollen and black. There was some blood in a stream on the ground about a foot long. There was also blood oozing from her mouth, nose and ears.'

Forty-two-year-old Sarah Chesham of Clavering might have got away with her crime had she not fallen out with her best friend. Hers was not the brutal solution of axe or rope, but the quiet, yet equally final way of the poisoner. A farm labourer's wife with six children, she had been pregnant by the time she got married at nineteen. In 1847 two of her sons, James and Joseph, died in agony, vomiting copiously. Poisoning was suspected, and post-mortems revealed traces of arsenic in both bodies. Sarah was charged with their murder. Amid rumours of an affair, one Thomas Newport, a Clavering farmer, was suspected and arrested for aiding and abetting her. However, the evidence, it was judged, was not conclusive, and she was acquitted. It has also been suggested that a Quaker on the jury did not agree with the death penalty.

Then, three years later, in May 1850, it was the turn of Sarah's forty-three-year-old farm labourer husband Richard to die following a long illness. He was buried at Clavering church and tongues started wagging. Richard Chesham had succumbed to lung disease, but with intermittent bouts of violent pain and sickness. Had Sarah been poisoning again? Arsenic poisoning is a slow and painful way to die.

Small traces of arsenic were found in his body – but again, the evidence was inconclusive and again Sarah was set free.

Sarah's friend, Hannah Phillips, often complained about her husband. 'Phew!' Sarah is said to have told her. 'I wouldn't live with such a man.' She then proceeded to dish out some helpful advice on the best way to poison an unwanted relative. Villagers had a name for the two conspirators; they called them both 'Sally Arsenic', though nothing could be proven against them.

The Devil smiles when friends fall out – and the two women did. Hannah Phillips told the authorities about the advice she had been given by Sarah: 'She told me to bake a pie of liver and lights, and she would provide a special seasoning of poison, which would dispose of my husband.'

It spelled the end for Sarah Chesham. Her husband's body was exhumed and a bag of rice, laced with arsenic, was found in her home. Yet it was not her husband's death she was charged with this time, but the attempted murder of Hannah's husband. So, third time unlucky, she was hanged, the last woman in Britain to be executed for attempted murder.

Unlike the Drory case, there was no repentance on her part, not even in her final moments. Thomas Drory took three minutes to die; Sarah Chesham clung on for seven.

Joining in the 'entertainment' of the crowd outside Springfield Prison on that fateful day of Tuesday, 25 March 1851, *The Times* noted 'hawkers of ballads' with 'true and correct accounts of the execution' and 'all kinds of edibles appeared'.

The printed ballad sold at Thomas Drory's execution declared: 'I in a field did her entice/ And with a rope I did her kill.' Sarah Chesham's poetical inspirations were slightly more lurid:

On the twenty-eighth of May,
The wretched woman she did go
To a shop to buy the fatal poison,
Which has proved her overthrow.

JOSEPH MORLEY'S UNCONTROLLABLE IMPULSE

He had a morbid interest, so she was foully murdered ...

He was only seventeen, just 5ft tall and barely 8 stone, but James Berry, his executioner at Chelmsford Prison, allowed a drop of 7ft. Death was instantaneous. A terse statement in *The Guardian* of 16 November 1887 concludes:

> In a confession of his guilt Morley states that the crime was not premeditated, but in cutting Mrs Bodger's throat he yielded to an uncontrollable impulse. He further states that he was led to commit the crime in consequence of his reading an account of the recent clerical murder in Suffolk, and that he had long taken a morbid interest in perusing narratives of murders and crimes.

Reader, Beware!

Martha, wife of James Mears Bodger, a gardener, was twenty-four years old and still abed at Beale's Cottages, Romford Road, Barkingside, nursing her six-month-old baby. Her husband had taken a cup of tea up to her before leaving the house early for his place of employment. He later remembered he heard 'the six o'clock Epping horn' as he walked to work. Downstairs he had left their lodger, blacksmith Joseph Morley, partaking his breakfast. Shortly after 6 a.m. loud screams were heard by neighbours, coming from Mrs Bodger's bedroom. The door being locked, the husband was sent for. As he rushed upstairs he found his wife:

> ... lying across the bed in a pool of blood. There was a fearful gash in her throat, and her hands were also cut. There was blood all over the room, and on the walls; also in the prisoner's bedroom and downstairs. On the floor near the deceased

THE DEADLY SHOEMAKER

William Calcraft (1800-1879) was born in Little Baddow on 10 October 1800. Trained as bootmaker, his life-changing experience came while he was selling pies outside Newgate prison on hanging days, when he made the acquaintance of Foxton, hangman in the city of London. It led to Calcraft's employment at Newgate, flogging juvenile offenders at 10 shillings a week. Calcraft was sworn in on 4 April 1829. It proved to be a busy year for the new hangman, with no fewer than thirty-one executions. On occasion he employed an assistant.

Calcraft put to death some 430 or 450 people, including at least thirty-five women, using the 'short drop' method, i.e. his clients would only fall about 3ft, which was not always enough for a quick death. Sometimes the condemned person would not die and Calcraft had to go below and hang on to their legs to stop them struggling. Sometimes, during executions, he would play to the crowds ...

Remuneration was a guinea a week retainer, plus a guinea a drop at Newgate, besides half a crown for every man he flogged and an allowance for cats (cat-o-nine-tails) or birch rods. In the provinces he could charge more per hanging, usually £10, plus expenses. As perks he would sell the victims' final belongings to Madame Tussauds to clothe the latest gruesome exhibits in their gallery of horrors. The hanging rope would sell by the inch afterwards and the more notorious the victim, the more he could earn. He was the most prolific hangman in Victorian England, and the longest serving.

In 1851 William Calcraft performed a double execution at Chelmsford prison, using his 'short drop' method. Thomas Drory and Sarah Chesham were the unfortunate recipients of his services.

William Calcraft, Britain's most prolific and longest serving hangman (forty-six years) was born in Little Baddow.

was found the broken handle of a razor, and the blade was afterwards discovered under the carpet.

It was the husband's razor, which the lodger had taken from its usual place.

There was one saving grace in that room of horror: the Bodger's baby daughter was left alive. As her father explained:

> I told my neighbours she was murdered, and they said, 'Oh, never,' and asked, 'Is the child dead?' I then ran upstairs, and saw the little thing in the bed laughing at me. I took it away from its mother's arms. I saw that my wife was quite dead. The child was covered with blood. I took it into the next-door neighbour's.

Joseph Morley denied everything, but the evidence against him was overwhelming. At the police station he was stripped, and blood was found on his clothing. Part of a neckerchief 'with blood on it' was found in the soil of the closet (the privy), while the other part was still in his pocket. He, too, had cuts on his fingers.

Inspector Saunders described the position in which he found the body of the deceased: 'The head was nearly severed from the body. There were two cuts on the fingers of the left hand. The bed and floor were covered with blood, and there was every appearance of a struggle having taken place.'

An 'attempt at violation', as the prosecution put it at Morley's trial, was the motive, but it had gone horribly wrong. Morley's obsession with the deceased had changed to rage. 'The victim [was] a young married woman, well known and much respected in the neighbourhood', reported Lloyd's *Weekly London Newspaper*.

Mr Justice Field had the odious task of putting on his black cap in the densely crowded Chelmsford courtroom and condemning Morley to death, despite

his age. The execution took place at 8 a.m. on Monday, 21 November 1887. The convicted lad submitted quietly to the pinioning by Berry, and walked to the scaffold without assistance, but sobbing all the time. There had been a tearful goodbye from his father two evenings earlier.

'YOU SHOULD HAVE HIT HER WITH YOUR FISTS, DAD, NOT WITH THE AXE.'

When her daughter found Mary Crawley's body on a bed 'with the brains hanging out', the Crawley's son John admonished his father Michael with the words: 'You should have hit her with your fists, not with the axe.' Arguments had been the *status quo* in the Crawley household in Wells Street, Stratford, East London. We can infer from the son's comment that domestic violence was frequent, only this time it had got out of hand. Sixty-two-year-old Michael Crawley had hit his wife twenty times over the head with an axe – and all over a penny's worth of nails.

After wandering around Barking Marshes for 24 hours, Crawley gave himself up. His trial took place in July 1847. Counsel's suggestion that manslaughter was the proper verdict, as Crawley had attacked his wife in a frenzy whipped up by her 'passionate' character, was dismissed by the judge in his instructions to the jury. The Home Office rejected a recommendation of mercy based on Crawley's advanced age. He was hanged on Friday, 23 July 1847, outside Chelmsford Prison.

ANOTHER CUT-THROAT MURDER

Jealousy can gnaw away at a person, eventually turning an unwarranted suspicion into uncontrollable action. Twenty-six-year-old Charles Finch had conducted himself with valour in the Crimean War. However the idea that his girlfriend Harriet Freeborn had cheated on him with another suitor in London during his absence would become an obsession that would be his undoing upon his return.

The former lovers were walking in a field near the village of Rivenhall when he decided to avenge that perceived slight to his dignity. He produced a cut-throat razor and sliced the young lady's throat. It cannot have been remorse that made him flee the scene, for he soon returned to cut her throat twice more ... He then sat calmly down, awaiting his arrest. He was hanged outside Chelmsford Prison on Wednesday, 29 July 1857.

'So help me God, I am innocent!'

When the Royal Victoria Dock and sundry industrial estates were still known as Plaistow marshes in east London, a shooting party found the headless, naked body of a man. The head was found the following day. It belonged in life to Theodore Furhop, a German, and it was another German who was arrested for his murder. Ferdinand Kohl, a sugar refinery worker on the Thames, had known the deceased for some six weeks. Both the police and the prosecution were convinced that the motive was robbery.

The trial at Chelmsford Assizes lasted just two days. Kohl had to be handcuffed in the death cell following a suicide attempt. Even as the trapdoor opened and the noose tightened at Chelmsford on Thursday, 26 January 1865, the condemned was heard to cry: 'So help me God, I am innocent!'

THE SLAYING OF A POLICE OFFICER

Thirty-eight-year-old Inspector Thomas Simmons, together with a constable, were going about their business looking into a burglary on a farm near Romford when they noticed three known burglars watching an isolated house. The suspicious trio, James Lee (forty), David Dredge (fifty-two) and James Martin were hiding in a hedge when the law enforcers approached. Shots were fired and Inspector Simmons fell, mortally wounded. He died four days later.

Lee and Dredge were apprehended and sent to the Old Bailey. Dredge successfully claimed not to have been a part of the schemes of Lee and Martin, though he admitted being present. He was found not guilty. Lee was sent to Chelmsford, guilty of murder, to be hanged at the prison on Monday, 18 May 1885.

James (or John) Martin got away, but did not change his ways. Short of nine months later he was hanged at Carlisle, Cumbria, together with two accomplices, following a burglary and violent attempts to escape.

MURDER AT THE ADMIRAL ROSS

Cecilia Jane Crozier, thirty-one years of age and newly wed to fifty-three-year-old Samuel Crozier, landlord of the Admiral Ross Inn at Great Baddow, had simply fallen off the sofa and died 'of natural causes', according to her husband. The explanation was accepted and Cecilia Jane was duly buried. It seems the doctor who signed the death certificate had missed the bruises and injuries which had really caused her death a day after the 'fall'.

Shortly after the funeral, however, witnesses came forward, giving a quite different account of events. Samuel Crozier had knocked her off the sofa, kicked her and beaten her repeatedly, they said. That

The crowds press ever nearer to the gallows.

was what had killed her. The publican was arrested on 28 June 1899 and charged with her murder. He was hanged at Chelmsford Prison on Tuesday 5 December that year.

THE WORK-SHY PIMP OF PLAISTOW

William Burrett married his meal ticket in May 1900, when he was twenty-nine and she was twenty, having lived with her – and off her immoral earnings – in Plaistow, East London, since she was fourteen. Ada Gubb was a full-time prostitute and apparently happy to carry on as a street worker even after the wedding. Obviously she wasn't quite the doormat he had thought her to be, though, for now there was a condition: 'It's about time you got a proper job,' she told him. 'If you don't do something about it, I'm giving up on the game.'

Burrett saw red. He went berserk, grabbed a knife and stabbed her so often and so viciously that he practically disembowelled her.

Neighbours came running in response to her screams, but they were too late. Ada Gubb could not be saved. She died in hospital that same evening. During Burrett's trial at the Old Bailey the judge ordered all women to leave the courtroom – the medical evidence was horrific. The murderer's plea of provocation was thrown out of court. William Burrett died at the gallows of Chelmsford Prison on Wednesday, 3 October 1900.

THE CHRISTMAS EVE MURDER OF 1910

Out of nine all-male executions in Chelmsford in the twentieth century, two were the result of wife murders and six had, as their victims, girlfriends or ex-girlfriends.

George Newton, a gas worker, murdered his twenty-one-year-old sweetheart Ada Roker at Stratford on 24 December 1910. The couple were engaged and about to be married in the first week of January. He had no reason to be jealous. Everyone agreed they seemed to be happy together, though they quarreled frequently and Newton had mentioned that he felt he couldn't trust Ada.

Ada's mother was about her business as flower seller, but there were other people in the house. Only for a short while had they been alone ... There was no scream before Newton rushed out of the house. Ada's brother stated in court: 'I was in my room on Christmas Eve when I heard Lizzie screaming and I heard her say, "Oh, George, what have you done?" I went into the kitchen and saw my sister lying there dead.'

Lizzie was their twelve-year-old sibling. Newton had been lodging with his brother-in-law, Henry Allen. In evidence, Allan recalled that on that fateful evening he had been asked into the front room by Newton, where:

> ... he handed me a razor; it is my razor, which I kept in the kitchen table drawer. I have never known him to take it before. When he handed it to me it was stained with blood. I said, 'What is the matter with you? What have you done?' He said, 'I have cut Ada's throat.

The police surgeon's evidence painted a horrific picture:

> Just in front of where she was lying there was a patch of blood on the floor; there was another patch of blood on the other side of the table, and also blood across the table. I examined her throat, and found a cut extending from behind the left ear down to the bone, about an inch and a half beyond the middle line of the body; very considerable force must have been used. I do not think the wound could have been self-inflicted; it could have been caused by the razor produced.

What was it, on that Christmas Eve, that made Newton snap? According to his brother-in-law's testimony, he must have gone to his fiancée's house prepared to kill, with the razor in his pocket.

Several cases of insanity in his family were cited in court, but the accused's calm and reserved behaviour made this look irrelevant. Nor was the jury's plea for leniency in consideration of the killer's youth taken into account.

George Newton was hanged by John Ellis and William Conduit on the 31 January 1911 in Chelmsford. He was only nineteen.

ZULUS ROUT LORD CHELMSFORD,

or the Massacre at Lion Mountain!

WHEN LORD CHELMSFORD'S column returned to the foot of the mountain that looked like a lion, they found a sight of horror: whilst they had been out hunting the Zulu army in the Mangeni Valley, the Zulus had attacked their base camp. Few remained alive to tell the tale – redcoats and drummer boys alike lay slaughtered in the sun. The corpses had been stripped and disembowelled. Some had been skewered to the ground with the deadly assegai stabbing spears – called iklwa, from the sucking noise they made when pulled from an enemy's body.

Other standard Zulu weapons were skull-smashing knobkerry clubs, throwing spears and shields made of cowhide. If a Zulu warrior did not 'wash his spear' in the enemy's blood, he went without sex. The Zulus impi formation of attack was called 'the beast's horns'. Representing the head of a buffalo, young warriors made up the 'chest' at the centre of the front line, and the 'horns' then swept around both flanks to encircle the enemy. This had happened at Chelmsford's base camp.

Another contingent of some 4,000 veteran Zulus had attacked the hundred soldiers of B Company, 2nd Bt., 24th Foot guarding Rorke's Drift.

The gruesome sights were even discussed in Parliament back home. After all, the defeat at Isandlwana was the worst debacle suffered by the Empire in any colonial war.

The man who led the British contingent on behalf of Parliament in January 1879, with 3,500 soldiers – armed with state-of-the-art Martini-Henry breech-loading rifles and two 7-pounder artillery pieces, as well as a rocket battery – was Lt-General the Rt Hon. Frederic Augustus Thesiger, 2nd Lord Chelmsford.

Frederic's father inherited a valuable estate in the West Indies, but that was destroyed by a volcano; he then settled on a legal practice in London. He was

Frederic Augustus Thesiger, 2nd Baron Chelmsford GCB, GCVO.

AFTERMATH OF THE ZULU VICTORY

✖ When news reached London of the massacre on Lion Mountain, Lord Elcho spoke in the House of Commons Debate on 27 May 1879: 'He gave the Zulus credit for their gallantry; but he had seen a letter which showed them the type of man they had to deal with in that country … and the writer said that every soldier who fell was disembowelled; that the hands, feet, and heads of many were cut off; and that drummer boys were found with their hands tied behind their backs and hung up on meat hooks.'

In most accounts of the aftermath at Isandlwana it is the drummer boys who are mentioned especially as examples of Zulu atrocities:

✖ Samuel Jones of the 45th Regiment recalled: 'One sight, a most gruesome one, I shall never forget. Two lads, presumably two little drummer boys of the 26th Regiment, had been hung up by butcher hooks which had been jabbed under their chins, then they were disembowelled: all the circumstances pointed to the fact they had been subjected to that inhuman treatment while still alive.'

✖ Trooper Thomas Henry Makin, 1st (King's) Dragoon Guards, stated: 'The first we saw was a little drummer boy, his drum broken in, his head cut off and placed on his chest, his hands inserted between his ribs. We then came across the poor fellows laid in groups of 5 and 6, every one of which had been mutilated by those savages and all were laid naked, every article of clothing having been torn off them. We came across a large wooden structure like a double scaffold, where two other boys had been hung up by their hands to the hooks and as they had decomposed, their bodies had fallen to the ground where they lay, with no friendly hand to give them a decent burial.'

✖ Another eyewitness remembered: 'A drummer boy threw his sword at a Zulu; he was caught, tossed in air landing on the assegais.'

'called to the Bar' on 18 November 1818. Six years later he distinguished himself in several high-profile cases and in 1832, at Chelmsford Assizes, he won a hard-fought case after three trials – to which he attributed so much of his subsequent success that, when he was raised to the peerage, he chose to be created 'Baron Chelmsford' of Chelmsford. Among his later job descriptions were King's Counsel, Solicitor General and Attorney General for England and Wales, and Lord Chancellor.

His eldest son, Frederic Augustus Thesiger, 2nd Baron Chelmsford GCB,

Lord Chelmsford, sketched in the field by a fellow officer.

GCVO (31 May 1827-9 April 1905), earned distinction as a soldier and became a general. At Isandlwana, at the foot of the Lion Mountain, however, he was to meet his match: despite a vast disadvantage in weaponry, the numerically superior Zulu overwhelmed and killed more than 1,300 troops in Chelmsford's absence.

Cetshwayo, King of the Zulus, had sent the 24,000-man strong main Zulu army on 17 January to meet the intruders with this command to his warriors: 'March slowly, attack at dawn and eat up the red soldiers.'

Chelmsford had so underrated the Zulu opposition that he had not bothered to entrench when they pitched camp at Isandlwana on 20 January, and no circle of wagons was formed. Instead, he divided his force, taking about 2,500 men, including half of the British infantry contingent, and setting out to find the main Zulu force. Little did he know that it was waiting for him at his own base!

At the height of the Zulu attack, on 22 January 1879, a solar eclipse was interpreted by the Zulu impi as a sign and an omen of their victory. No quarter was given to the British regulars in their red coats, who fought back-to-back with bayonet and rifle butts to the last. Of the 1,700-plus force of British troops and African auxiliaries, about 1,300 were killed, most of them Europeans, including the field commanders. Some 1,000 Martini-Henry rifles, two cannons, 400,000 rounds of

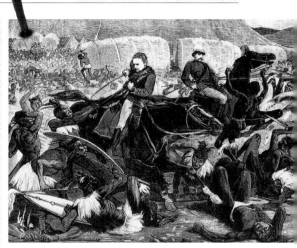

The Battle of Isandlwana. (Illustrated London News)

ammunition, most of the 2,000 draft animals and 130 wagons, as well as tinned food, biscuits, beer, overcoats, tents and other supplies fell to the victors. The Zulus had lost around 1,000 killed; the number of wounded is not known.

By the time Chelmsford's successor arrived in Africa, Chelmsford had won other smaller victories over the Zulus and was exonerated in despatches. Of his four sons, the eldest later became Viceroy of India and first Viscount Chelmsford. Another son, Lieutenant-Colonel Eric Thesiger, was a Page of Honour to Queen Victoria and he also served in the First World War.

AD **1880**

THE GREAT FLOOD

'**D**URING THE WHOLE of Saturday night there was a tremendous and incessant downpour of rain, and on Sunday morning all the streams in the district, including the Chelmer, the Can, the Wid, and the Navigation River, rose very rapidly, and overflowed their banks, vast expanses of land being under water. The valley of the Navigation all the way from Chelmsford to Maldon, a distance of ten miles, presented the appearance of an extensive lake.'

So began a news report by *Essex Newsman* of the awful floods of 16 October 1880.

On the Sunday morning, several Chelmsford men were involved in the rescue of bullocks and horses at Baddow Meads: Frederick Marriage (senior and junior); William Joseph Brown, farmer, dealer and blacksmith of Stock (who owned some twenty stranded horses); Mr Jesse Brown of the Plough Inn, Chelmsford; Herbert Markham of the Duke's Head Inn, Springfield Road; Mr Munn, farmer of Stock; and several unnamed others.

Seven or eight bullocks were rescued, but the horses were running in all directions: though they might have run along the inundated and invisible banks of the stream for great distances, they always avoided it instinctively. Not so the humans.

Answering a call for help, Mr Brown 'tucked up the tails of his coat' and stepped too far to the left and fell into the stream. He wore 'a greatcoat buttoned up and this sustained him in the water'. In reaction to his cry for help, a man called Boultwood ran towards him – and also fell into the stream. He reached Brown and managed to turn him over, but then he himself sank out of sight. Frederick Marriage senior and junior were standing near the mill and witnessed the men drowning: throwing off their hats and coats, they took the reins from Mr Brown's horse, which was standing in a trap nearby, and threw them out from the towing path. Sadly, Mr Brown did not seem to see them (or was too exhausted to react). Thinking quickly, Marriage senior fastened the reins about his son's waist. Junior jumped into the water and just managed to grab hold of Mr Brown as he was sinking, 'the hair of his head only being visible'. Poulter and Brown's son stood up to their waist in water as they helped, pulling him to safety. He was put into his cart and his son took him to the Duke's Head, where he was attended to by Mr Pitts, the surgeon. He made a rapid recovery.

The unfortunate Boultwood, who had sacrificed himself to save Mr Brown, was a married man with seven children, four of them still at home. His body was not recovered until late Monday morning, when it was taken to the Three Cups Inn, Springfield, to await an inquest. Two of the troublesome horses died in the floods;

WHEN CHELMSFORD'S CHURCH FELL DOWN

As Chelmsford's parish church, St Mary the Virgin's origins probably reach back in time to the beginnings of Chelmsford itself. It was rebuilt in the fifteenth and early sixteenth centuries, but on Friday, 17 January 1800 disaster struck when workmen dug inside the church, carrying out the time-honoured tradition of burying notable citizens inside the hallowed environment. The nearest pillar supporting the roof was undermined, taking down other pillars in the south arcade and with them the roof, the south aisle and part of the north aisle. Rebuilding took three and a half years, during which time services were held in the Shire Hall. It must have been an auspicious start to the new century, especially as the town was still awash with soldiers of the Napoleonic Wars.

The 1801 census counted 3,755 Chelmsfordians.

When the new Anglican diocese of Chelmsford was created in 1914, the parish church of St Mary the Virgin became the cathedral. In 1954, the cathedral was additionally dedicated to Saint Peter and Essex's own Saint Cedd.

'East View of Chelmsford's Church (now the cathedral), that fell on the 17th of January 1800,' when St Mary's Church at least partially collapsed. Mercifully there was no loss of life. (Image courtesy of Chelmsford Museum)

the others were recovered alive from the Meads that Monday morning.

In Chelmsford proper the floods extended from the Stone Bridge, up the High Street to the entrance to the London Road and from the London Road Bridge to Tindal Street, where most of the cellars and cellar kitchens were flooded. Gardens and ground floors of some of the houses in the vicinity of the two rivers were inundated. In the London Road the water reached high enough to put out kitchen fires. Outbuildings were smashed, trees uprooted, wheelbarrows, timber and casks went down the Can and the Chelmer. Chickens had to be raked out of the water and tame rabbits just floated away. Water rushed up from the drains, which were unable to cope. The Queen's Head yard and others were flooded. Low-lying land surrounding Messrs Beach's oil mill in the fields between Chelmsford and Writtle was inundated and the men could not get to work on Monday morning. On Sunday morning the night watchmen had been rescued by horse and cart.

The inquest upon the body of John Boultwood, a farm bailiff aged forty-nine, was held at the Three Cups Inn, Springfield Road, on the Wednesday morning. There Mr Brown agreed that had it not been for the swift action of the Marriages, he would have perished: 'I shall be indebted to him (young Marriage) as long as I live.' The quick-thinking Frederick Marriage, senior, was also the father of thirteen children. Marriages owned most of the mills around Chelmsford. What happened to the hapless would-be rescuer's family was not recorded.

The news report added that the most disastrous flood in human memory at the time had been in 1824, 'when most of the streets in the town were flooded and a large portion of Moulsham was submerged. The Stone Bridge was then believed to be in great danger.'

Barnes Mill c. 1930. It was owned by the Marriages.

THE DASTARDLY MOAT FARM MURDER,

or the Missing Miss Holland!

'**S**AMUEL HERBERT DOUGAL, you are charged in this indictment that on the 19th day of May, 1899, at Clavering, in the county of Essex, you feloniously, wilfully, and of your malice aforethought did kill and murder one Camille Cecile Holland. How say you: are you guilty or not guilty?'

The words of the Clerk of Arraigns at Chelmsford's Shire Hall, at the Essex Summer Assizes on Monday, 22 June 1903, started one of the most celebrated criminal cases of the early twentieth century.

The prisoner replied: 'Not guilty.' But the evidence against him was overwhelming. Before the court stood Samuel Herbert Dougal, a man with the air of a 'captain' of the armed services, a title he preferred to be known by – Captain Samuel Dougal – but which he had never actually earned or achieved. He had, however, served a time in the army, which culminated in the position of Chief Clerk in the Royal Engineers. During his nine years service in Halifax, Nova Scotia, he managed to lose two wives in quick succession. His Welsh-born first wife of sixteen years died in June 1885 after a short illness. His second spouse, whom he married just two months after the first Mrs Dougal's demise, enjoyed less than two months of wedded bliss, before she too died on 6 October that same year.

On leaving the army in 1887 Samuel Dougal's life had its ups and downs.

While working in Dublin he was sentenced to twelve months' hard labour for forgery. Following attempted suicide, he spent time in an asylum. He was, however, more successful with the opposite sex and there were a number of liaisons, before he made a hit in London when he courted a spinster with a small invested fortune of some £6,000 or £7,000 and a bank account in Piccadilly.

Camille Cecile Holland also owned a fair amount of furniture and articles of jewellery, mainly inherited from an aunt with whom she had lived until her bereavement. Samuel had plans for that money, finding an isolated farm in Essex, Coldhams Farm near Clavering, for them to set up home. The purchase was paid for by Camille (£1,550, plus £300 for the stock on the farm), a place large enough to take her furniture and books, etc, but the little lady insisted it was bought in her name. 'Captain' Dougal renamed it Moat Farm and 'Mr and Mrs Dougal' moved in on 22 April 1899.

A maid was engaged on 13 May. Florence Havies (later Blawell), found herself in the kitchen on her first morning at Moat Farm, being kissed by her new employer. She went and told her mistress. In the night of 16 May the young woman had to hold her door shut against Dougal while she yelled for her mistress, who came and stayed with her on that and consecutive nights.

Moat Farm at the time of the crime. The small dog pictured belonged to the victim, Camille Holland.

On the evening of 19 May, Miss Holland and Samuel Dougal went out for a drive in a pony and trap, dressed, but without luggage. 'Good-bye, Florrie, I shan't be long,' the lady told the maid. However, Miss Holland was never to return.

Later on, Dougal returned – on his own. The mistress had gone to London, he said; he would fetch her back from the train later. He went out again several times that night, ostensibly to meet trains, but the mistress did not return. The alarmed girl spent the night fully dressed, sitting up against her door, only to find Dougal up and about at breakfast time, declaring he had a communication from Miss Holland which stated that she had gone on a short holiday and would send another lady in her stead.

However, this story did not ring true: it was impossible to get to London and back in a single day, and impossible for the note Dougal claimed to have received to have arrived so early in the morning. The maid wrote to her mother and left that very day. The 'friend' Miss Holland was supposed to have sent was actually Dougal's wife number three, who immediately moved in.

All ran smoothly for a while: a new maid was engaged, and Dougal became a pillar of the local community (albeit with a few local dalliances thrown in) – until, that is, his arrest on 27 April 1903. Money had left Miss Holland's accounts as if she were still attending to her finances. Her signature had been forged. It was a crime without a body, and a desperate hunt began – ended when police dug up a ditch close to the house, which had been filled in about the time of Miss Holland's disappearance, almost five years earlier.

Camille had been shot at close range and simply dumped, fully dressed, into the ditch before it was filled in. The bullet was still lodged in her skull and matching bullets and a gun were found at the farm. There was not much left of the body, but the fifty-six-year-old's distinctive shoes and clothes were identified by those who made them or worked on them. She had been a remarkably petit woman, with a very small shoe size. Her furniture was still at the farm and was identified by relatives.

Samuel Herbert Dougal was executed by hanging at Chelmsford prison at 8 a.m. on Tuesday, 14 July 1903, and buried in the prison grounds. A number and his initials are his memorial on a wall close by.

THE EXPLORER AND THE SAS

IN ITS 280 years of existence, the Grade II listed Hylands House grew with the fashions and fortunes of its previous nine private owners until, in 1966, Chelmsford Borough Council purchased house and park for the community.

In 1726 local lawyer Sir John Comyns bought the manor of Shaxstones in Writtle. Here, on the high land, he built his family home. Alas, the family did not materialise, and the house went to a nephew, John Comyns of Romford, who left it to his son, John Richard Comyns, in 1760.

Thirty-seven years later, in 1797, Danish merchant Cornelius Hendrickson Kortright acquired it at auction for the princely sum of £14,500. More land was bought and the house enlarged. Defensive fortifications during the Napoleonic Wars (1803-1813) at nearby Galleywood brought Hylands' first connection to war and the military, a connection soon strengthened: in January 1810, the *Essex Herald* remarked of Kortright's hospitality: 'an elegant ball and supper at his beautiful seat Highlands ... at which all the fashionables in the neighbourhood were present, including many military gentlemen'.

In 1814 Pierre Caesar Labouchère, having prudently withdrawn from Dutch merchant banking and the money markets of Amsterdam, purchased the estate. When the newfangled nearby railway disturbed his peace, he almost bank-rupted the company with a compensation claim. His son Henry sold Hylands to the upwardly mobile entrepreneur and MP for Harwich, John Attwood, formerly the owner of an ironworks in Birmingham. His largess in improving and enlarging the estate and his status eventually bankrupted him and he died in France, a pauper.

The new owner, Arthur Pryor, partner in the Truman, Hanbury and Buxton Brewery, rebuilt the church at Widford and erected a completely new one in the racecourse at Galleywood, all with brewery money. Hylands at that time employed in excess of twenty-one servants. Arthur Pryor's son rented out.

Sir Daniel Fulthorpe Gooch, 3rd Bt, purchased Hylands House in 1907. Shooting parties and fêtes, grand weddings and receptions, were regular Gooch

Hylands House today.

Hyland's owner, Sir Daniel 'Curly' Gootch on the Endurance, *second row centre (in dark attire), seated next to Ernest Shackleton in his flamboyant hat.*

family entertainments. Some 700 guests were invited to celebrate King George V's Coronation in 1911.

In 1914 an advert appeared in a London newspaper: 'Men wanted: for hazardous journey. Small wages, bitter cold, long months of complete darkness, constant danger, safe return doubtful. Honour and recognition in case of success. Sir Ernest Shackleton.'

The explorer was seeking men to sail with him on the *Endurance* on his Imperial Trans-Antarctic Expedition. The idea was to cross the Antarctic and be met by another ship, which would sail from Australia.

There was no shortage of volunteers, but war was imminent and the man who had been chosen to take charge of the dogs on *Endurance* rejoined his regiment. At the last moment Shackleton turned to an old friend whose qualifications as a dog handler were breeding hounds for the hunt, though he was a keen and experienced yachtsman. Sir Daniel Gooch (nicknamed 'Curly') signed on as an able seaman.

War clouds were gathering. After sailing from London, on Monday 4 August 1914 Shackleton went ashore in Kent to find that general mobilisation had been ordered. Immediately he offered the ships, stores and services to the country. Winston Churchill returned his telegram with thanks, but desired that the expedition go ahead. On Tuesday the King handed Shackleton a Union Jack to carry on the expedition. War broke out that night, at midnight. On the following Saturday, *Endurance* sailed from Plymouth for Buenos Aires.

Shackleton and the sledge dogs sailed separately from Liverpool on a faster ship and joined the *Endurance* in Buenos Aires, but the kennels were built during the voyage. On 26 October they sailed on to South Georgia, where Gooch left the expedition, returning home on 3 December 1914 – with severe frost bite, it is said.

In the meantime his home had been requisitioned as an emergency hospital by the War Office, opening on 14 August with ninety-five beds, under 2nd and 3rd South Midlands Field Ambulance, Royal Army Medical Corps. Some 1,500 patients would be treated here. In their blue hospital uniforms they came to be known locally as 'the blue boys'.

Sir Daniel had the most modern medical equipment installed, at his own expense, and Lady Mary was a commandant among the nursing personnel. Fêtes were held to raise funds for the Essex Regiment's prisoners of war, when Lady Gooch and her daughter served tea in the marquee, while games and sporting events were underway. Both King George V in 1914 and Lord Kitchener in 1915 reviewed the troops in the park.

Death strikes far and wide and indiscriminately: the Gooch's eldest son, Lancelot Daniel Edward Gooch, as an eighteen-year-old midshipman on active service in the Royal Navy, serving on HMS *Implacable* in the Dardanelles, fell ill and died in Greece in 1915. Hylands hospital closed again in 1919 and an 'Armistice and Demobilisation Dance' was held to celebrate the ocassion.

The house reconnected with the brewery in 1922, when it was bought by John Hanbury, chairman. He died suddenly before even moving in and Hylands was left to his wife Christine and their son Jock. A private area in the gardens was dedicated not only to the memory of her husband, but later also to that of her son, when again war took its

Wounded soldiers at Hylands House Hospital in 1918. (Reproduced by courtesy of the Essex Record Office–I/ Mb 403/1/47)

THE SAS AND THE WAYWARD JEEP

Mrs Hanbury, it appears, accepted the wartime invasions, as well as regular invitations to dine in the Officers' Mess, but she had her limits.

When Captain Paddy Blair Maine, founder member of the SAS and this country's highest decorated soldier, as well as one of the most famous folk heroes of the war, drove a jeep up Hylands' grandiose internal staircase for a bet, she was not amused. Roused by the commotion the incident provoked, Mrs Hanbury is said to have thrown open the doors of her chambers and confronted the boisterous SAS men with the words: 'Gentlemen, I believe you have taken a wrong turn.'

She then ordered the culprits to bed, with instructions to remove the Jeep in the morning when they had clearer heads. The Jeep had to be dismantled before it could be removed from the first-floor landing.

A heavily-armoured jeep patrol of 'L' Detachment SAS, wearing Arab-style headdress, 18 January 1943. (Courtesy Imperial War Museum)

---

toll on a Hylands' family. Pilot Officer Jock Hanbury, with 615 (County of Surrey) Squadron, was killed in 1939 when his plane crashed during a night-flying exercise.

Christine Hanbury opened the estate to organisations like the Red Cross during the Second World War, just like previous owners had in times of need. Troops manoeuvred in the grounds prior to the Crimean war; it served as a hospital in the First World War, and a German Prisoner of War camp was established during the Second. A wireless command post for the 6th Anti-Aircraft Division was set up – and then, in 1944, it became SAS (Special Air Services) headquarters.

The SAS is still remembered with tales of hidden weapons and ammunition that 'were hastily buried to avoid the embarrassment of handing back more than had been issued when the Regiment was finally disbanded at Hylands'. It's no idle folklore. A Chelmsford Borough Council press release of 2004 revealed: 'Yesterday, workers in Hylands Park discovered old looking, rusty boxes of bullets – about 30 or 40 magazines, flat tins, rifle cleaning kits, .45 ammunition and the barrel of a BREN gun, buried in the ground behind the park toilet block situated near the Writtle car park.' The Council's men had been laying water pipes in the park when they hit upon a trench containing the stash. Essex Police were called, who 'cordoned off the area and alerted the Army Bomb disposal experts'. The surplus items were removed and incinerated.

CHELMSFORD IN THE SECOND WORLD WAR

IN 1940, GERMANY'S planned Operation Sea Lion, the invasion of the United Kingdom, depended on air and naval supremacy. That was thwarted in the Battle of Britain and the idea was postponed indefinitely on 17 September 1940.

As an important centre of light engineering, Chelmsford's factories became obvious targets of the Luftwaffe in the Second World War, both for aircraft and missiles – but, as was so often the case, it was civilians that were hit.

The Marconi Co. employed more than 6,000 people in Chelmsford, producing important military communications equipment, so it is perhaps not surprising that the New Street factory became a target for bombs in May 1941. The death toll was seventeen lives.

A monument in the cemetery on Writtle Road stands to the memory of workers killed in two raids on the New Street factory of Hoffmann Manufacturing Co. Ltd during the Second World War. The worst single loss of life occurred on Tuesday, 19 December 1944, when the first 367th Vergeltungswaffe 2 – or V-2 – rocket to hit England fell on Henry Road, a residential street near the Hoffmann's ball-bearing factory and not far from the Marconi Wireless Telegraph Co.'s factory. Thirty-nine people lost their lives and 138 were injured, forty-seven seriously.

Several houses in Henry Road were completely destroyed and many were badly damaged in the surrounding area.

It was a time when women went out to work to replace the men who were needed at the front, food and clothes were rationed, and everyone carried their identity

Hoffmann's ball bearings found extensive use, keeping wheels turning in both World Wars, so much so, that German bomber pilots were issued with maps that specially outlined Hoffmann's factory (marked 'd', top centre). Target location/ identification image issued to Luftwaffe bomber aircrew prior to bombing raids on British towns and cities during the Second World War.

Guglielmo Marconi's factories were blitzed during the Second World War. (LC-USZ62-77563)

card and gas mask wherever they went. Originally gas masks contained asbestos, so we can be grateful – for if the bombs did not get you, eventually the asbestos would.

What German bombs could not manage in wartime was finally achieved during the summer of 1990, when most of the factory was demolished. The sprawling Rivermead Campus of the Anglia Ruskin University now occupies the site. Chelmsford's defence-related industries have all but vanished. Instead, its closeness to London and its central Essex location have favoured it greatly as an administrative and distribution centre and as a commuter town. Chelmer Village was built in the 1980s. Some of the Hoffmann remains have been converted into luxury apartments and a health club. Beaulieu Park, 'The Village' and Chancellor Park are some of the more recent large-scale housing developments.

The Marconi Co. has a strange history. We still read and hear of flying saucers, and there are still people who insist they have had contact with alien species, been abducted or transported mysteriously to outlandish places. And it's not all that long ago that people did not believe wireless communication was possible, let alone its worldwide application. So it is hardly surprising that early last century, when a young Italian came to England and

conducted his experiments in wireless transmission and reception, people suspected all sorts of possible repercussions.

Guglielmo Marconi arrived in 1896 at the behest of the General Post Office to demonstrate his 'wire-less' invention. Experiments in this new and complex tampering with the unknown continued apace amid trials and errors, constantly widening the range of transmissions. In 1897 he formed the Wireless Telegraph & Signal Co. in London.

Following the transmission of signals across the English Channel in 1898, commercial development of the Italian's apparatus began in earnest in December that year in an old factory he had bought, an abandoned Silk Mill in Hall Street, Chelmsford.

On 12 December 1901 Marconi bridged the Atlantic by transmitting signals in Morse code from Poldhu in Cornwall to St John's, Newfoundland. The expanding company moved into a purpose-built radio factory in New Street, Chelmsford, in 1912, next to the Great Eastern Railway. A railway siding ran across New Street into the factory yard and brought materials in one end of the works and took finished radio equipment out at the other.

At the South end of the building two huge aerial masts once stood: the 450ft (137m) high 'Marconi Poles' formed Chelmsford's most prominent landmark. Work done here, in its laboratories and workshops, established a worldwide radio telegraph system for the Government. The world's first short-wave radio equipment was developed and the BBC was set up to control the public broadcasting pioneered by Marconi – the first broadcast programme was made here in Chelmsford. Dame Nellie Melba sang the first entertainment radio broadcast from Marconi's factory.

The crackling sounds that came over the ether mysteriously from great distances away opened up new possibilities, scary to some, but exciting to many. Mass communication had arrived. Crystal sets became popular in the 1920s and few homes were without a wireless set by 1930.

But old ingrained beliefs that the 'canals' on Mars had been dug by an intelligence like ours or maybe greater than ours persisted, and many now found the possibility of contact promising or perhaps worrying. When atmospheric interference problems were reported, theories were rife and word went out that it was the good citizens of Mars who were frantically attempting to get in touch with us earthlings. Was there intelligent life out there in the great unknown? Were the imagined aliens friendly or belligerent?

The writer and artist Donald Maxwell recalled an episode in 1925 of some three years earlier:

> It was during the time when mysterious interferences had been felt at various wireless stations in Great Britain and elsewhere, and the startling theory had been adopted by some newspapers that possibly the planet Mars was trying to signal to the earth. The possibility of these interferences coming from outside our world had been admitted as just possible by Signor Marconi.

Well, why shouldn't that most earth-like of planets also be the home of earth-like creatures who might want to try and catch our attention? Maybe their planet was dying?

Doing Fleet Street's bidding, Maxwell was hurriedly despatched from London to Chelmsford by train on a dull and miserable winter's morning, to provide a double-page sketch for the centre of the paper 'without committing yourself or the *Graphic* [the newspaper in question] to any theory about these mysterious signals'.

'How on earth,' he later recalled, 'I could draw wireless disturbances coming from Mars or anywhere else I had not begun to get any glimmering of an idea.'

Maxwell's worries subsided somewhat when he actually saw the wireless station: 'the giant masts with their multitudinous wire stays, the medley of blocks and insulators, and the great concrete anchors gave promise of something mysterious in its suggestion. By dragging in Mars and the moon I might succeed in giving an impression of something eerie going on in the night ... I would wait for moonrise.'

A sign of tumultuous times left behind – pill boxes south of Chelmsford.

Maxwell's view of Marconi's 'otherworldly' apparatus. Chelmsford wireless station, c. 1922.

If you enjoyed this book, you may also be interested in…

Haunted Chelmsford

JASON DAY

Much of the more sinister history of England took place in Chelmsford and it would seem that many of the participants, and victims, of these events still haunt the town today. Join author, broadcaster and paranormal investigator Jason Day as he introduces you to the ghost of an angry nun, a phantom theatre guide and a spectral cyclist. Encounter the 'Box Monster', the spirits of those women falsely accused of witchcraft. Dare you read on to discover these and many more ghosts of Chelmsford?

978 0 7524 6221 9

Murder & Crime: Essex

MARTYN LOCKWOOD

This chilling collection of true stories delves into the villainous deeds that have taken place in Essex during the last 100 years. Cases of murder, robbery, poisoning and fraud are all examined as the shadier side of the county's past is exposed. Compiled by a former Inspector with the Essex Police Force and illustrated with a wide range of photographs and archive ephemera drawn from the archive of the Essex Police Museum, *Murder & Crime: Essex* is sure to fascinate both residents and visitors alike.

978 0 7524 6083 3

Bloody British History: Bury St Edmunds

ROBERT LEADER

Starting with the Saxons and moving swiftly on to the vicious murder of King Edmund by a Viking horde (though he quickly got his revenge on his killer when he returned as a weapon-wielding spectre), the attack on Abbot Lofestan (whose hands were withered in an act of holy retribution) and a whole host of battles, riots, plagues and scandals, this is a shortened history of the town with all the boring bits snipped out. With more than 70 illustrations, you'll never look at local history in the same way again!

978 0 7524 6287 5

Essex Ghost Stories

ROBERT HALLMANN

Set in the historic county of Essex, this gripping compilation includes stories of restless Vikings; the mysterious haunted picture of 'Cunning' Murrell, the last witch doctor in England and foul murders. amongst others. Robert Hallmann interweaves historical fact and reported ghost sightings with imaginary events to create perfect tales for reading under the covers on stormy nights. Illustrated with charcoal drawings and the author's own eerie landscape photography, this book will enchant readers time and again.

978 0 7524 4848 0

Visit our website and discover thousands of other History Press books.

www.thehistorypress.co.uk

The History Press